Eliot's Reflective Journey to the Garden

Eliot's Reflective Journey to the Garden

by

Marion Montgomery

The Whitston Publishing Company
Incorporated
Troy, New York
1979

ACKNOWLEDGMENTS

Portions of this work, sometimes in different form, first appeared in the
following periodicals: *The Arizona Quarterly; Georgia Review; Illinois
Quarterly; Intercollegiate Review; Renaiscencc: Essays on Value in Literature; South Atlantic Bulletin; South Carolina Review; Southern Review;
Southwest Review; T. S. Eliot Newsletter.*

For Tom Landess and Bill Provost

TABLE OF CONTENTS

Table of Contents

There are three conditions that often look alike
Yet differ completely, flourish in the same hedgerow:
Attachment to self and to things and to persons, detachment
From self and from things and from persons; and, growing be-
    tween them, indifference
Which resembles the others as death resembles life,
Being between two lives—unflowering, between
The live and the dead nettle.

Little Gidding

That was a way of putting it—not very satisfactory:
A periphrastic study in a worn-out poetical fashion,
Leaving one still with the intolerable wrestle
With words and meanings.

East Coker

These are only hints and guesses,
Hints followed by guesses; and the rest
Is prayer, observance, discipline, thought and action.
The hint half guessed, the gift half understood, is Incarnation.

Dry Salvages

INTRODUCTION

"Then Eliot caught religion," the student paper says. "The sow caught the measles and she died," I respond. From what did he catch it, how long a period of incubation, is it the last infirmity a poet is subject to? Those are the interesting questions. This book attempts some answer to those questions. It is about Eliot's mind, as any serious book about him must of necessity be. We shall be concerned with the conditions and circumstances of his life, with the personal, which must refer somewhat to the surface spectacle of Eliot's life—his routine labor at Lloyd's Bank, his difficult first marriage, his "nervous breakdown" which led him in a flight toward recovery at Lausanne, where most of *The Waste Land* was composed. But our concern will be to distinguish the surface spectacle of his circumstances from the deeper event of which *The Waste Land* is a record, the major symptoms of Christianity he was "catching."

In one view of Eliot's symptoms, he may be said to have exhibited its pains and agues from very early. At the turn of the century, poets like Eliot and Pound found themselves in strong reaction to contemporary poetry in English, and the consequence was that they began to take words seriously. Inevitably when one does so, he becomes entangled in metaphysical problems, for he must attempt to reconcile words to existence. In the wake of the struggle for a concept of reality which would sustain and justify that act of refinement and elevation of language which we call poetry, the "schools" began to emerge, choosing names for themselves that advertise their solution of the word's relation to the desert each found himself an inhabitant of: *imagist, vorticist, objectivist.* Pound on many occasions in the early days attempted to recruit Eliot to a movement. Yet one does not find Eliot in the ranks of any particular school. His attempt to find "the word neither diffident nor ostentatious," through which to establish "an easy commerce of the old

and the new" led him inexorably to the Word. But that is a slant
upon Eliot's journey which we see from its end, since "the end
is where we start from." It says little of the uncertainty of his
struggle along the way. When one starts backward from the
end, seeing the chosen roads in retrospect, what had seemed
uncertain in each moment of the passage appears as inevitable,
and the roads not taken peripheral. The difficult choices along
that way were to appear happy ones only at the time of the
Four Quartets, having led as they did to the Word.

Religion is not a disease, however convenient and general
that supposition has been to modern thought. There is a difference between infective conditioning and learning, though not
always made in our concerns with the mind. Any perceptive
teacher knows from his experiences the difference between the
student assuming the role of an object to be conditioned and the
student devoted to learning from the kinds of questions the
mind is capable of. The one asks, "Is this going to be on the
test?" The other asks, "What does this mean?" The one says
on the test. "Eliot caught religion in 1927 in *For Lancelot
Andrews.*" The other does not answer but asks why, though he
too is likely to know the date of Eliot's essays announcing a
turning. The difference between conditioning and learning
is that in learning there is a giving of the will to a possible knowing and being, a willing suspension more active than "disin-
terested" suggests. It is for such a student, whatever his condition of servitude in relation to a mind more inclusive than the
ego, that the journey of this essay is intended.

Out center of concern is Eliot's mind as it is reflected in
The Waste Land and in the manuscript of that poem now recovered, through which document we see Eliot's divergence from
many of his contemporaries; for in *The Waste Land* he turns
from the terror of his own existence to the terrors accompanying the acceptance of Him in Whom we live and breathe and have
our being. We are dealing, then, with the supernatural, at its
first level with the existence of mind—awareness as it discovers
its faculties and certifies its materials. Mind, even the human
mind, is in the region of the supernatural, as Eliot's fellow
Anglican C. S. Lewis has affirmed in his defense of *Miracles.*
For those who are reluctant to grant that direction to mind,
among them many of Eliot's contemporaries who saw his poem
as a betrayal of the intellect's hard-won independence from the

supernatural, one may remark of the two alternatives to that position that a belief in the natural or the subnatural is hardly a satisfactory solution, leaving more questions unanswered than are asked. Those who have the most difficulty accepting the supernatural, with its conception of Absolute Being and the implication of potential human existence deduced from it, seem little troubled by the leap of faith which turns to the Absurd—to the accidental and subnatural—attracted it would seem to a conception of nonexistence, nonbeing, and pursuing that conception with what must also be described as religious fervor.

As to the third alternative, faith which accepts mind at the natural level, excluding either the Absurd or the Supersurd, it would seem a position possible at this old age of the mind only in the interest of a pragmatic determinism which has so remarkably left its stamp upon the natural and which seems therefore to certify its validity as ultimate. But again, Francis Bacon leaves much unanswered, and those marks on nature become a cause of increasing panic in our day as we consider the effects of our empirical interest upon the four elements among which we exist: earth, water, air, and fire. Such a mind as Bertrand Russell's, which assumes itself the most advanced point of civilization in time and is so emotionally concerned with the prospect for the future, can only envisage that future as characterized by "a world without poverty, without war, with little illness." It does so, looking to "human science" (whose dark potential Huxley and Orwell have figured for us in their fiction) as a precision instrument to adjust the individual and "undo the evils which have resulted from a knowledge of the physical world hastily and superficially acquired." Having divested himself early of the belief in free will, Russell is left with the only possible evil as ignorance, to be remedied by the only absolute, human science —through education, that most dangerous of words. One is arrested by such simplistic faith as Russell's, which can assert in the 1960s that "education could produce without much difficulty" the conditions the world needs if it is to survive: "tentativeness, as opposed to dogmatism, in our beliefs; an expectation of co-operation, rather than competition, in social relations; a lessening of envy and collective hatred."

Human existence limited to the natural level—with its creed of Humanism outworn—seems hardly to answer the necessities of the mind, for it denies the reality of that discontent which Eliot calls *desire* in his poem. To justify the restlessness by elevating mind as its own first and final cause, to see the health of the mind as a matter of adjustment into the body and of the body into nature's clock, does not answer that desire, any more than running back the clock in spring saves us daylight. (The joke about the extra week in September made up of Daylight Savings is an incisive one.) The approach to mind which holds that it exists merely at the natural level can create a temporary illusion of having answered the problem of desire. That illusion spawns religious fanatics out of such men as Freud or D. H. Lawrence, who are taken as first prophets in the overthrow of the mind that the body may be elevated for worship. It is not a direction so far removed from that power of empiricism vested in the "Establishment" as the revolts of Alan Watts and Allen Ginsberg pretend, they being rather the Calvin and Wesley of Protestant Empiricism as Ralph Nader is its Billy Sunday. When we come to the bottom of the disagreement, the argument between the orthodox and protestant factions turns out to be over how to worship the world and the flesh, not whether. The interests in communes, in a drug culture, turn out to be an attempt to turn back the clock as protest against the exploiters who would run it ahead.

There is a fourth alternative position, the undecided, so numerous that from Dante's and Eliot's report one would not suppose death could have undone so many. It is really about these that we shall be largely concerned, because Eliot was so largely concerned with that state of his own mind. Prufrock is the most immediate instance in Eliot's poetry, but not the only one. The undecided mind is the one we wake from as we cease to be among the numbers of the uncommitted, as Eliot woke himself and as he dramatizes in his work—prose and verse alike, and in varying degrees of innocent and knowing revelation. In that movement forward we measure through narration to a new location of the mind such as this essay wishes to address: that of the pilgrim-student who makes the gesture, who gives the will to possibility. Through that gesture, in Eliot's experience of it, one discovers the shadow removed which otherwise falls between motion and act, between emotion and response.

But *motion, movement, location,* with an inescapable implication to art of what Eliot calls the "narrative mode," are but a necessary surface language through which we try to talk about the mystery of a metamorphosis of being deeper even than that "mythic mode" of *The Waste Land* is capable of disclosing. It is a change in Eliot to be measured from his early pronouncement of the conditions of Ante-Hell, in which the impossibility of saying just what we mean makes cowards of us all, to his late announcement of one's constant condition, *in time*, of Ante-Purgatory, where one's own shadow is "huddled by the fire against the red rock." always in the condition of the late repentant anxious to assume the tortuous ascent before it and yet always fearful of anticipating its end through the will gone astray. In that anticipation, one presumes the future and is thrown into the past, and so is perpetually caught in time, struggling to escape time. "We never," says Pascal, "keep to the present. We recall the past; we anticipate the future as if we found it too slow in coming and were trying to hurry it up, or we recall the past as if to stay its too rapid flight. . . . The fact is that the present usually hurts." The only hope of desperate man is the continual dew of mercy through grace, the burden of Eliot's position after *The Waste Land.*

If it has been impossible to say just what one means in the earlier poetry in its attempt to project the disaligned self beyond its own borders, after 1922 the problem is deepened, though less burdensome to the self. Now a different witness is borne to a world not much given to the prospect of grace. It is not so burdensome, since the grace of this new "Calling" waters for Eliot "the inner freedom from the practical desire" (*Burnt Norton*) and makes possible a "release from action and suffering," that plagueful dilemma of Prufrock. In such release, time ceases to be the enemy it always has been to poet or philosopher, for now Eliot believes that the still point he desired from of old is "not the intense moment/Isolated, with no before and after,/But a lifetime burning in every moment" (*East Coker*). Action and suffering, those incompatibles that Aristotle attempts to reconcile in his conception of tragedy, are reconciled for Eliot in that moment of Passion which consumes all moments of time, the intersection of the world called the Incarnation. It is a Passion which one must imitate, as St. John of the Cross has it, and Eliot presents his version of that imitation in "Ash-Wednesday." There, action and desire are reconciled to suffering and memory, and released in what he will call in *Little Gidding* the "last gift" that is "reserved for age": the "rending pain of re-enactment/Of all that you have done and been." It is an abiding purgatorial moment, as long as earthly life, which is "not of action or in-action" (*Dry Salvages*), but a condition of simplicity that allows one to discover how the perpetual darkness may be "the light, and the stillness the dancing" (*East Coker*).

A seemingly dark and sober view of the human condition, not to say mysteriously contradictory to the usual sight, for mystery is contradiction of the known except in the vision of the mystic. But it is not finally so dark a vision as it seems from the outside, as is evidenced by Eliot's gaiety in his daily life. More and more that gaiety comes to the surface, through memoirs such as Bonamy Dobree's and in Eliot's letters that find their way into print in increasing numbers. It is worth our noting that when Eliot has come to accept the hard lesson that "Sin is Behovely" (*Little Gidding*), he can write his book of practical cats. For it was finally possible to Eliot to see cheerfully that "every phrase and every sentence is an end and a beginning,/ Every poem an epitaph." That is a comfortable reassurance in *Little Gidding,* whereas the ghost of that same idea which haunts the early poetry could only cause terror or despair. It is this idea that prevents an action of words in Prufrock, to whom the word unsaid, unspoken, seems the only means of self-preservation. Eliot comes to see inaction as a form of death in life, but he does not react extremely. He writes Bonamy Dobree in 1927, "I suppose the only thing to be done about W. Civilisation is to think as clearly as one can." He is capable of marching through London's inner City to protest the threatened demolition of its historic churches, singing "Onward, Christian Soldiers" and other hymns, but he does not remove himself from that city's life. Defending his choice of epigraph from St. John of the Cross for his *Sweeney Agonistes,* the writes Dobree:

> The doctrine that in order to arrive at the love of God one must divest oneself of the love of created beings was thus expressed by St. John of the Cross, . . .a man who was writing primarily not for you and me, but for people seriously engaged in pursuing the Way of Con-templation. . .merely to kill one's human affections will get one nowhere, it would be only to become rather more a completely living corpse than most people are.

One may observe that the natural affections of a Sweeney are scarcely to be distinguished from animal affections, but the danger of such a decline does not justify one's divesting himself of the love of created beings and things. Such action might be to do a possibly right thing for the wrong reason, leaving one in the spiritual condition of "the sable presbyters" of "Mrs. Eliot's Sunday Morning Service," who are rather oblivious of devout souls burning invisible and dim on the one hand and of the bees engaged in the "blest office of the epicine," on the other. After *The Waste Land,* there is an increasing effort on Eliot's part to think as clearly as one can, in order to avoid an extreme action which out of ignorance often establishes the opposite of its intent. Eliot's labor may well appear timidity to those who do not see as Eliot does how the Puritan attempt to force every man to divest himself of the love of created things rather has the effect of establishing materialism as the new god.

As the address of my arguments so far hints, the essay which follows is a multiple creature of my own mind. It contains literary criticism, including explication of Eliot poems I have not dealt with, or dealt with in a different focus, in my *T. S. Eliot: An Essay on the American Magus* or my more recent study of *The Reflective Quest for Order in Dante, Wordsworth, Keats, Eliot and Others.* It contains some literary history, in particular attempting to set Eliot against his background and examine his relation to Pound beyond what I have done in the two books mentioned or in my *Ezra Pound: A Critical Essay.* It contains excursions into ideas and arguments of philosophers and theologicans: Pascal, St. Augustine among them, and among moderns some questioning of Russell, Whitehead and Brice Parain. It argues in part that Eliot did not want his biography written since he had already reported the significant personal in his essays; by implication therefore this essay is itself the sort of biography of which Eliot would seem to approve. But it goes beyond that: it enjoys exhortation and rebuke and expects response in kind. In short, it is an essay whose justification lies not in the virtues of scholarship of a purer kind, which it does not eschew, but in the play of mind upon interesting minds— the principal justification of the *essay* as opposed to the more exacting requirements of philosophy or theology or literary and historical scholarship of the purer strain. What I would hope to accomplish is an enlivening of that mind which is willing to engage me here, to the end that it will reject, correct, purify, enlarge or establish what it encounters. If one find opportunity to exercise each of these pleasures of the mind through these

pages, I shall be content.   I publish it because I am confident
that no one of those pleasures alone will serve the purpose.

I

ELIOT AND "IL MIGLIOR FABBRO"

Footfalls echo in the memory
Down the passage which we did not take. . .

Burnt Norton

We have lived with Eliot's public version of *The Waste Land* for fifty years, proliferating commentary and exegesis in an attempt upon its history and meaning so that we might determine whether it is a poem or sequence of poems, or a fragmentary ruin; whether a masterpiece which reorders the world's masterpieces, as Eliot instructs us to expect of the new masterpiece, or merely a chimera conjured out of our age's need to justify itself on the stage of literary history. The result has been that commentary, exegesis, and gossip have well-nigh buried the poem, so that at this point in its existence we feel safe in saying only that it (along with Pound's *Cantos*) is the most notorious poem of the century. There has hovered about *The Waste Land* from the beginning the shade of that other *Waste Land*, now materialized, the lost version from which Eliot and Pound extracted the poem we know. That the original version might turn up one day and dispel shadows—perhaps prove some combination of Dead Sea scroll and *Secret History of the Dividing Line* between the two great poets—was a constant expectation.

It was an expectation kept alive by Eliot's belated dedication of his poem to Pound, in 1925, the year Three Mountains Press published Pound's first substantial offering of the *Cantos*. The matter is still on his mind in 1938 when he remarked that

> the phrase, not only as used by Dante, but as quoted by myself, had a precise meaning. I did not mean to imply that Pound was only that [the better craftsman] : but I wished at that moment to honour the technical mastery and critical ability manifest in his own work, which had also done so much to turn *The Waste Land* from a jumble of good and bad passages into a poem.

That dedicatory phrase, *il miglior fabbro,* is fraught with ambiguity nevertheless, and increasingly so as we reflect that Eliot's literary allusions are complexly metaphorical. Their correspondences radiate from the center of the particular words and phrases he borrows outward to the literary and historical context of his sources, and inward to Eliot's own poems and to his deepest life. That borrowing from Dante's XXVI Canto of the *Purgatory* must lead us to reflect that it is a favorite passage, which Eliot has gone to before, having chosen a phrase from the same lines as the title of his second collection of poems, *Ara Vos Prec.* He returns to the same sentence of that Canto for a telling phrase in "Ash-Wednesday," IV: "*Sovegna vos.*" The phrases together: "Now I pray you, be mindful [in due season of my pain]." It is now perhaps that due season. Eliot knew that his dedication of the poem to Pound as *il miglior fabbro*—to one who "forged with yet greater skill his mother-speech"—is not only public gesture, but a semi-private one as well. For the phrase he chooses is not literally from Dante's text, but adapted by Eliot to the occasion; it is literally borrowed from Ezra Pound's *The Spirit of Romance,* where it stands as the chapter title of Pound's celebration of Arnaut Daniel. Given the dedication's ultimate source in Dante, near the summit of Mt. Purgatory, and remembering that Dante places the words ("*fu miglior fabbro*") in the mouth of an admired poet of love (Guido Guinicelli) in order to praise an innovator even more devoted to love poetry (Arnaut Daniel), we must read the circumstances carefully.

As an example of the error one falls into when the context is not carefully considered, we have recently Professor David R. Rebmann's warping of the source to suit his thesis (in a letter to the *Times Literary Supplement,* February 11, 1972, p. 156). Professor Rebmann accounts for Daniel's position on *Purgatory* as being "because he was a hermaphrodite," the brush he is intent on tarring Eliot with. (One presumes he means bisexual.) In point of fact, Dante is quite careful to distinguish Guinicelli (the Eliot of our dedicatory metaphor) and Daniel (the Pound) from the Sodomites who race about the seventh cornice in a direction *opposite* that of Guinicelli and Daniel, who are among those guilty of natural lust. (See lines 40-48, XXVI, *Purgatorio.*)

The exchange occurs in the region where excessive love of the world and the flesh is expiated. The ultimate source of the words is, of course, Dante, who sees himself the superior of Guinicelli and Daniel, at the point of going beyond them in his understanding of love, on to an encounter with Beatrice in the earthly paradise.

We are dealing with a poet whose working title for his poem is "He Do the Police in Several Voices," a sentence from Dickens' *Our Mutual Friend.* Eliot has a reputation as a playful mimic among his friends. (Herbert Howarth reports, in his *Notes on Some Figures Behind T. S. Eliot,* that "it is said that, weekending with friends, he will read Dickens aloud, entering the characters with his voice," and he took special delight in imitating the Cockney maid he and Vivien employed for a time.) And so we may begin to suspect that Eliot's dedication of his poem to "a better craftsman of his mother-tongue" implies rather careful limitations. That Eliot is capable of whimsy and playfulness in the midst of his most serious concerns is the "possum" in him, which on occasion irritates Pound. "Tom" Eliot, as his friends called him, in the midst of the agonized self-inspection of his "Portrait of a Lady," at a point where he is looking into the heart to unravel its dark mysteries, could speak of his literal pulse in the ear with the playfulness of a Donne:

> Inside my brain a dull tom-tom begins
> Absurdly hammering a prelude of its own,
> Capricious monotone
> That is at least one definite 'false note.'

And he could also, in that more intense concern with the dark night of the soul, use his literal journey in the London subway as the term of his metaphor, in that paragraph of *Burnt Norton* beginning:

> Descend lower, descend only
> Into the world of perpetual solitude,
> World not world, but that which is not world,
> Internal darkness, deprivation
> And destitution of all property...

The longer one reads Eliot's poetry, the more firmly he becomes convinced of the multitude of things going on in words and phrases, in a range from the playful to the deadly serious. Nor is it easy to draw a fine line between what is intentionally present, what accidental and irrelevant, and what is present as discovery and so not appropriately included by either the intentional or the accidental. In dealing with a reflective poet, one must necessarily engage the dangers of the intentional fallacy and affective fallacy. Indeed, those are aspects of the creative process which engage Eliot again and again as he looks back upon his own poems. We are not thereby licensed for a wild goose chase after Taro cards, and we shall certainly be foolish in pressing "round behind the gashouse" to yield a St. Louis baseball team, the old "Gashouse Gang." And yet we must, perforce, look into intention and discovery. What shall be our safeguard? Good sense, however ambiguous that phrase, and a confidence in our subject's integrity and intelligence. We may make some justification of that attitude by looking briefly at the concern for the source of the title Eliot finally uses instead of his working title, "He Do the Police in Several Voices."

With the publication of the manuscript version, the question of the source of Eliot's title to that poem is raised again, in the letters column of the *Times Literary Supplement,* in March 3, 1972 and March 17, 1972. Is it from Jessie Weston's book, or directly from *Le Mort d'Arthur*? And was the seed of that phrase planted in his youth, perhaps from reading Sidney Lanier's popular *Boy's King Arthur*? One might suggest also Madison Cawein's "Waste Land," published by Harriet Monroe in *Poetry,* Volume I, pages 104-105, a poem which yeilds interesting comparisons. It is highly probable that Eliot was familiar with all of these, certain that he knew some of them. But source hunting in Eliot which does not recognize a particular genius in Eliot as poet is barren: he had a gift for the striking phrase or image or idea which reverberates in the history of his and his reader's minds, and because it touches common intellectual experience it is likely to touch sources even Eliot may not have encountered directly. If the emotion poetry is concerned to stir must be, in his phrase and with his emphasis, *"significant emotion,"* its signs—its material forms—must be significant as well. That is, those materials must relate significantly to the memory and desire of the restless mind, which is not confined to any epoch. He is a reflective poet, and where there is continuing light the reflective mind continues to image forth, more largely than it may itself have consciously contained.

My argument has dangers, since it would seem to destroy precision in a poet devoted to purifying language and making it precise; it would seem to sanction any and every reading. But in fact it does not; it assumes Eliot's a true vision, not a unique one. The correspondences between such diverse minds as Augustine's (*The Confessions*), Baudelaire's (*Flowers of Evil*) and Eliot's

(*The Waste Land*) are remarkable, but inevitable, since each mind is turning toward the same Light. It is the validity of that Light which is the final concern and which justifies the correspondences.

Given the serious poet, we may observe that his poem may mean more and less to him after he writes it than it seems to do at the time he writes it; Eliot says much the same of his own poetry in the *Four Quartets.* And similarly with sources. To bring the two together, consider the difference the following passage can hold for the poet of the "Preludes" and "Prufrock," engrossed in problems of phenomenology, from what it can mean to the poet of "Ash-Wednesday." How early did Eliot read Pascal? In his student days on the Continent, he was reading widely in Frence literature under excellent tutelage, even as he had already read Dante. It is unlikely that he was ignorant of the work of such an important mind. Number 545 of Pascal's *Pensées,* the work in which Pascal is setting his own house in order, is a paradigm for the struggle Eliot's *Waste Land* discloses, but written at an elevation Eliot was to reach only with "Ash-Wednesday." The final concern, as we see in Eliot's essay on Pascal, is not whether Eliot borrowed from Pascal, but that he found Pascal true. Number 545, in A. J. Krailsheimer's translation, reads:

> 'All that is in the world is lust of the flesh, lust of the eyes or pride of life.' *Libido sentiendi, libido sciendi, libido dominandi.* [I John 2:16] Wretched is the cursed land consumed rather than watered by these three rivers of fire! Happy are those who are beside those rivers, neither immersed, nor carried away, but immovably steady beside these rivers, not standing but sitting, in a low and safe position. They will not rise thence before the light, but, after resting in peace, stretch out their hands to him who shall raise them to stand upright and steady in the porches of Jerusalem the blessed, where pride shall no more be able to fight against them and lay them low; and yet they weep, not at the sight of all the perishable things swept away by these torrents, but at the memory of their beloved home, the heavenly Jerusalem, which they constantly remember through the long years of their exile.[1]

As we look into Pound's contribution to the final form the poem assumed for public show, we may be prepared to appreciate Eliot's relation to his collaborator. In many respects they are like-minded and their names go in tandem in the history of modern poetry in English. But there are fundamental differences which each recognized in the position of the other, differences which later led to caustic public remarks, as in Eliot's examination of Pound's Hell of the *Cantos* (in *After Strange Gods*) and in Pound's irritated references to Eliot from time to time in the *Cantos*. That they could share such intense excitement over the prospects of Eliot's manuscript and yet each maintain his independence is a tribute to the integrity of each as man and craftsman. One conclusion we may anticipate: *The Waste Land* marks a parting of the ways between them, though not a loss of friendship or esteem.

If Eliot seemed to Pound to be overly concerned with the mottoes on sun-dials, Pound may well have seemed to Eliot too much entangled by the elegance of Circe's hair. That entanglement is not one from which Eliot himself is exempt, but there lies an important difference: Eliot could not be content until he could reconcile the weeping lost girl who troubles him in "La Figlia che Piange," the girl with "her hair over her arms and her arms full of flowers," to the promises of the "Lady of silences/Calm and distressed/Torn and most whole" whom he comes to in "Ash-Wednesday," the Mother in whom the torment of "love unsatisfied" and "the greater torment/Of love satisfied" are reconciled. (It is worth noting on our way that the title of that early poem is the name of a statue recommended to Eliot's attention by a friend, a statue he failed to discover in the museum in Northern Italy he visited in quest of it about 1911.) Eliot's overriding concern from the beginning is with the unfolding "Rose of memory," and should we succeed in naming some historical Annette Vallon for such early poems as this and his "Portrait of a Lady," we will have missed the point entirely to suppose the identification answers the problem. For the problem Eliot is concerned with is to discover an enlightening response to his peering into the heart of silence. It is the concern of his dissertation on Bradley and phenomenology, as opposed to Pound's analogous work which is on the aesthetics of dealing with Circe's hair, his study of Romance literature, *The Spirit of Romance*. Eliot uses as an epigraph to "La Figlia che Piange" Aeneas's agitated interrogation of the country girl who confronts him on the shores of Carthage, who is in fact his mother Venus: "O maiden, how may I name thee." Aeneas has the veils lifted from his eyes at last, but no such revelation occurs in Eliot's poem. There is no name for the maiden in which beauty and truth are reconciled, Venus, Beatrice, Mary. One might read Eliot's poem as a version of Keats's encounter with the Grecian urn, with the difficulty added that Eliot's urn—the stone figure of a girl weeping, flowers in her arms—is present only by rumor and through the action of the disturbed "imagination" and "cogitations" that, while they "*still* amaze" (Keats's ambiguous word that Eliot dwells more and more upon in his poetry) at the same time "trouble midnight and the noon's respose." But more on this problem presently.

Our recognition of a parting of the ways between Pound and Eliot, which *The Waste Land* may be taken as the center of, may help us reconcile ourselves to their literary age. We may see that we do not name it primarily Eliot's, as Russell Kirk's recent book, *Eliot and His Age*, might tempt us to do, nor primarily for Pound, as Hugh Kenner's almost simultaneous book, *The Pound Era*, inclines us to do. It seems rather more likely that we shall properly call the first half of this century, in respect to letters in English, the Age of Pound and Eliot, indicating thereby the intellectual and spiritual struggles and confusions and partial triumphs which they so resolutely pursued, the one declaring his high calling the task of purifying the language of the tribe, the other repeatedly reminding us with the fury of an Old Testament prophet that to use the wrong word is to bear false witness.

NOTE

[1]Tout ce qui est au monde est concupiscence de la chair ou concupiscence des yeux ou orgueil de la vie: *libido sentiendi, libido sciendi, libido dominandi.*

Malheureuse la terre de malédiction que ces trois fleuves de feu embrasent plutôt qu'ils n'arrosent!

Heureux ceux qui, étant sur ces fleuves, non pas plongés, non pas entrainés, mais immobilement affermis sur ces fleuves; non pas debout, mais assis dans une assiette basse et sûre, dont ils ne se relèvent pas avant la lumière, mais, après s'y être reposés en paix, tendent la main à celui qui les doit élever, pour les faire tenir debout et fermes dans les porches de la sainte Jérusalem, où l'orgueil ne pourra plus les combattre et les abattre, et qui, cependant, pleurent, non pas de voir écouler toutes les choses périssables que ces torrents entraînent, mais dans le souvenir de leur chère patrie, de la Jérusalem céleste, dont ils se souviennent sans cesse dans le longueur de leur exil!

XXIII. Melanges *Pensées sur la Religion et sur quelques autres sujects.* Edited by Jean Steinmann. Monaco: Éditions du Rocher, 1961. pp. 349-350.

II

TOWARD ANOTHER INTENSITY

We must be still and still moving
Into another intensity. . .

East Coker

We now know that the lost version of *The Waste Land* has lain in the vaults of the New York Public Library for years, a point of some irony since it is in one of its aspects the modern world's great city peom. It is available to us now as a handsome object, though at an exorbitant price. It is indeed so imposing as to be reported in movie gossip columns as being, at the hands of Nevill Coghill, Elizabeth Taylor's favorite birthday present along with her husband's gift of the million dollar Krupp diamond. The student interested in the making of the poem may be disappointed that it is not within his reach, but he may take some pleasure at the kinship between his position and that of Eliot at the time of its composition, when Eliot was writing hopeful letters to John Quinn about his economic situation and Pound was attempting to organize a committee of patrons to rescue Eliot from his arduous labors for Lloyd's Bank.[1] At Lloyd's his task was to settle pre-World War debts between that bank and German citizens. He writes his mother, in a tone of mixed pride and apology, of his "important appointment full of interesting legal questions," which keeps him busy "trying to elucidate knotty points in that appalling document the Peace Treaty." (We are given such information by Valerie Eliot in her concise and most helpful "Introduction" to *The Waste Land* material, which traces the outer history of the poem's composition from 1915 to the death in 1924 of John Quinn, through whose foresight the manuscript was preserved.)

The mixed tone of Eliot's letter home suggests that he found himself in an ambiguous position more complex than in his earlier role at Lloyd's Bank. He has risen considerably from the lowly office Aldous Huxley describes to brother Julian in 1916, after calling on Eliot at his duties. Huxley reports him "the most bank-clerkley of all bank clerks. He was not on the ground floor nor even on the floor under that, but in a sub-sub-basement sitting at a desk which was in a row of desks with other bank clerks." Now, however, because of his command of languages and his orderly mind, he is hardly clerk, but an agent dealing with problems of international finance whose roots are in the recent war. And we remember as well that the war placed him in an ambiguous position too, making him subject to Bertrand Russell's scorn for not being pacifist and disquieted with himself as well at not being able to find how or when to participate in the war effort. To look back at that war through his task of settling financial obligations in Lloyd's behalf might well add a strain beyond the burden of using his literary gifts in such otherwise mundane tasks. We encounter a sardonic note from time to time in *The Waste Land,* and are sometimes surprised, if not jolted by the intrusion of exhortation, as in the second paragraph of "The Burial of the Dead" or the last three lines of "Death by Water." These notes may well be preliminary evidence of a difficulty Eliot had in controlling the "personal" dimension of the poem. To suggest more firmly what I mean, we might examine the presence of the sardonic at the end of the first section of the poem.

It has seemed very probable to me that the final lines of the final paragraph of "The Burial of the Dead" carry more personal burden of Eliot's associations with Lloyd's of London than we generally credit. He was in an ambiguous situation, as Pound was not, being supported by the very world Pound attacks for its corruption in *Hugh Selwyn Mauberly.* We reflect upon St. Mary Woolnoth's proximity to Lloyd's, and when we note that it keeps the hours, but "with a dead sound on the final stroke of nine," it echoes for us the emptiness of daily commercial London life of which Eliot was a willing part no less than the typist. At the beginning of office hours, the "I" of Eliot's poem hails Stetson and addresses him as one sharing a knowledge of mutual complicity in a profitable venture. Mylae, a great Roman naval victory in the trade wars with Carthage, is an appropriate echo for Post-World-War-I London. Stetson is addressed as an old comrade of that war of aggrandizement, in a familiar and public manner, but in figurative (and cryptic) language. There is a flippancy in the tone of address which suggests that the true content of the language might run something as follows: "We know something these listeners [readers] don't, eh? You spoke last year of buying into Krupp. Was it really the sure thing you thought? Forgive me, old friend, but I can't help knowing. In such business, one can't help discovering the dog in the manger, eh?" The final line opens completely upon the dead world by including not only the speaker and Stetson in the vaguely sordid situation but the reader as well, by the introduction of that chilling line from Baudelaire: "You! hypocrite lecteur,—mon semblable,—mon frère!" The irony of the passage lies in the false implications of the imagery of planting, sprouting, gardening—with the planted corpse—which have seemingly to do with growth out of decay, until a sudden frost. But to talk of fertility myths in relation to the passage hardly answers our questions about this uncomfortable encounter in the Unreal City. We may reflect that in a chaotic but specialized world, the only common language has its roots in earth life—seasons and death—which seem rapidly deserting city folk. But there is no common signification possible in Baudelaire's city as Eliot encounters it in 1922. The language possible to the city poet engages Eliot as a problem from the beginning, as in his arresting juxtapositions such as the "twisted branch" and the "broken spring in a factory yard." Much later (1931) he will honor Baudelaire as having given "new possibilities to poetry in a new stock of imagery of contemporary life," by which he means the life of "a great metropolis." But in that late celebration he will emphasize most particularly a double vision possible to Baudelaire since he is "essentially Christian," through which interest he is able to elevate "such imagery to the *first intensity*" (Eliot's emphasis). Meanwhile, in 1922, there seems no common signification possible in that imagery, and even Madam Sosostris can't read the blank card the one-eyed merchant carries on his back. If she could—that is, if Eliot were willing to be more direct and didactic in the manner of Pound—we might well find the card inscribed "Usura: age-old and age-thick." And the silk-hatted Bradford millionaires might fall into the circle of our vision more clearly as war profiteers who dealt in woolen goods than they do in Eliot's simile.

Pound's urging Eliot into a marriage with Vivien Haigh-Wood is less fortunate to Eliot personally than his support of Eliot as poet and critic, though it is quite possible that the achievement of his poetry owes more to the misery of his eighteen years with her than he could know in that interval. Hardy, in circumstances similar to Eliot's, wrote, "If way to the Better there be, it exacts a full look at the Worst." It is exactly this approach to life that Eliot is to praise in Baudelaire, though he disclaims any kinship to Hardy. At the point where Eliot was about to bring himself to a final break with Vivien, he wrote of Baudelaire's difficulties with women that the French poet arrived "at the perception that a woman must be to some extent a symbol." If she is not Dante's Beatrice, Keats's Fanny Browne,

Hardy's Mrs. Henniker, or Yeats's Maude Gonne, she may well be Poe's Virginia Clemm or Baudelaire's Jeanne Duval or Eliot's own Vivien Haigh-Wood. The sense of Evil, says Eliot, implies the sense of good, though Baudelaire manages to confuse "evil with its theatrical representations" and never quite exorcises the "romantic idea of Love." Still there is in him "the reaching out towards something which cannot be had *in,* but which may be had partly *through,* personal relations. Indeed, in much romantic poetry the sadness is due to the exploitation of the fact that no human relations are adequate to human desires." Indeed, indeed. Even, one might add (as Eliot clearly sees by "Ash-Wednesday"), when the human relation, the romantic love, is of the self, a point of ironic concern in "The Death of St. Narcissus," discarded in his final revision of *The Waste Land.*

These are the considerations to which the second Mrs. Eliot, Valerie (in whom Eliot happily found his Maude Gonne), allows us further critical access by publishing the lost manuscript. We have before us the pages on which are Pound's and Eliot's and (occasionally) Vivien's annotations and emendations to prove the public version. What it does is underline more heavily the drama of a mind's struggle to come to terms with a world incidentally modern: a struggle to keep body and soul together in ways as fundamental as Plato's and Aristotle's and Augustine's questioning of the city, real and unreal. (That Plato and Augustine questioned the role of woman as symbol is too much a part of our thought to be developed at length.) The struggle is as prosaic and mundane as any man's attempt to pay his doctor bills, provide food and lodging, survive the real and imagined pressures of the nine-to-five press of office routine.

As to Pound's role, he refers to it as an "obstetric effort," and the degree of indebtedness Eliot feels to him is reflected by Eliot's desire in 1922 to publish Pound's notes and emendations with the poem. He wrote: "Wish to use Caesarean Operation in italics in front." To which Pound responds, "My squibs are now a bloody impertinence. I sent 'em as requested; but don't use 'em with Waste Land. You can tack 'em onto a collected edtn, or use 'em somewhere where they would be decently hidden and swamped by the bulk of accompanying matter. They'd merely be an extra and wrong note with the 19 page version." But in spite of his confidence in Pound, Eliot still feels an uneasiness about the poem as a whole. In addition to

"The Death of St. Narcissus," there are a number of excluded poems: a seventeenth-century "Exquy"; a Browningesque "Death of the Duchess"; a "Song for the Opherion"; a Bleistein-as-drowned-Phoenician in "Dirge"; an "Elegy." There are large sections of verses, untitled, also excluded, and Eliot enquires anxiously of Pound whether the excluded parts and poems ought to be published also. At the beginning if he simply must, Pound answers, but certainly not at the end. "I think your instinct has led you to put the remaining superfluities at the end. I think you had better leave 'em, abolish 'em altogether or for the present. If you *must* keep 'em, put 'em at the beginning before the 'April cruellest month.' The *poem* ends with the 'Shantih, shantih, shantih.' " It is a judgment with which there will surely be general accord, though John Quinn for one would have some of the discarded material included.

We can now appreciate, as Eliot could not at the time, what combination of causes led him finally to entrust the original manuscript to John Quinn, along with a provision that it not be published. It is "worth preserving in its present form solely for the reason that it is the only evidence of the difference which [Pound's] criticism has made to this poem." A second time he requests that the manuscript be kept private. "You will find a great many sets of verses which have never been printed and which I am sure you will agree never ought to be printed, and, in putting them in your hands, I beg you fervently to keep them to yourself and see that they are never printed."[2] Eliot surely knew the history of literary remains well enough to be aware that if they survive they are eventually published. He knew as well that his own manuscript contained some evidence of what F. W. Bateson, in a moment of anger against Eliot, speaks of as "primal idiocy."[3] But he could not bring himself to follow Pound's advice and "abolish 'em" absolutely, as Hardy destroys his first wife's diary or Eugene O'Neill his unfinished plays.

The poem is, after all, a document of the most personal of all experiences, a conversion, so that the personal and the historical inevitably impinge upon it, and the relation of the personal and historical to the aesthetic—in this instance, the poetic imagination—are large problems that Eliot confronts repeatedly in a public way (that is, in his essays), insisting that the personal be refined out, the historical subdued. Now we see better—as Eliot came to see—that *The Waste Land* reflects confusion as well as brilliance, the sweat and tears of a struggle at once privately spiritual and publicly aesthetic, cause enough to make its creator cautious beyond the possible embarrassments at the "primal idiocy" of their literary value. To destroy the manuscript would be at once to obscure the debt to Pound and a deeper rightness in the manuscript than Pound perceived. When we have looked somewhat into that indebtedness, we may proceed to the deeper rightness. That is, we may then consider why, in spite of the help now to be gained from the published manuscript, *The Waste Land* remains the great incomplete poem of our century, but incomplete in a sense quite other than may be said of the *Canterbury Tales,* the *Excursion,* or *Endymion.*

NOTES

[1]Miss Monroe had wanted to publish only parts of the poem, and was disturbed by the unresolved despair she saw in it. Pound writes a flurry of letters cajoling, scolding, shouting: "Your objection to Eliot is the climax . . . No, most emphatically I will not ask Eliot to write down to any audience whatsoever. . . Neither will I send you Eliot's address in order that he may be insulted." (November 9, 1914) " 'Mr. Prufrock' does not 'go off at the end.' It is a portrait of failure, or of a character who fails, and it would be false art to make it end on a note of triumph." (January 31, 1915) "No, if your committee don't make the award to Eliot, God only knows what slough of ignominy they will fall into—reaction, death, silliness!!!!!" (October 2, 1915) Pound succeeded in defending the integrity of Eliot's text but failed to secure him a prize, the Levinson Prize for the year ($200) going to Vachel Lindsay for his "Chinese Nightingale" and the Guarantor's Prize ($100) to Constance Skinner for "Songs of Coast Dwellers." If Eliot from this point in his career up to World War II was no longer to be ignored, neither was he so largely accepted as it sometimes seems. As late as 1939 such an influential anthologizer as Louis Untermeyer could bring himself to include in his *New Modern American & British Poetry* (New York: Harcourt Brace and Company) only the first twenty-two lines of "Prufrock"; "Morning at the Window"; and the first of Eliot's "Preludes." His introductory note characterizes Eliot as a momentary ripple on the surface of recent poetry: "As poetry, Eliot's expression was a bold and successful experiment to some, wholly incomprehensible to others." Some of his shorter poems, and passages "in the longer ones establish relations between beauty and the commonplace." In the volume an equal or larger space is devoted to the poetry of James Whitcomb Riley, Edwin Markham, Jean Starr Untermeyer, Richard Hovey, T. A. Daly. All of Eliot's poetry through *Burnt Norton* is published at the time.

[2]Quoted by B. L. Reid, *The Man from New York: John Quinn and His Friends.* New York: Oxford University Press, 1968, p. 540.

[3]*Essays in Criticism,* XIX, No. 1, p. 5.

III

PURPOSE BEYOND THE SEEMING END

And what you thought you came for
Is only a shell, a husk of meaning
From which the purpose breaks only when it is fulfilled
If at all. Either you had no purpose
Or the purpose is beyond the end you figured
And is altered in fulfilment.

Little Gidding

In early January of 1922, Valerie Eliot tells us in her introduction, Eliot stopped over in Paris to visit Pound. He was on
his way back to London from Lausanne, where he had gone to
place himself in the hands of "a specialist in psychological
troubles," as he phrased it a bit earlier. On his way home to
London and to Vivien he had with him fruits of those troubles,
the manuscript of that long poem he had wanted to write for
some time. As early as January of 1916, six months after his
marriage, he had written Conrad Aiken, "I have *lived* through
material for a score of long poems in the last six months." In
the interval the burdens of life had increased, the immediate
center of which seemed to be Vivien. She was, in those years
(as Pound writes John Quinn), "an invalid always cracking up, &
needing doctors," destined to become a greater burden before
she would be less. But Eliot was himself encouraged, having concluded from his own sojourn on the continent that there was
nothing wrong with his mind. The manuscript, parts of which
were written much earlier but the bulk of it at Lausanne, was
ample evidence that he had survived, as Pound is to affirm shortly in the mixed pride and envy of a godfather. "Complimenti,
you bitch," he wrote. "I am wracked by the seven jealousies,
and cogitating an excuse for always exuding my deformative
secretions in my own stuff." And after his "Sage Homme"
tribute in verse, beginning "These are the poems of Eliot/By
the Uranian Muse begot," he closes: "It is after all a grrrreat
littttttterary period."

It is an advantage in such a literary partnership when two
know each other's work and mind; when they share expectations
of poetry to a fine and refined degree, as Eliot and Pound did.
They didn't need to explain or detail objections. We do not
know what words were exchanged over the manuscript in Paris,
but many words would not be necessary. As for the manuscript
itself, as we have it, Pound needs only a squiggle in the margin
to indicate that "I look in vain" is wrong in Madame Sosostris'
mouth. Eliot changes it to "I do not find," giving an effect of
immediate intensity which the false *vain* prevents. And in the

same section there is a mark in the margin by a line from Revelations ("I John saw these things, and heard them"), a parenthetic interruption in conflict with the point of view which Eliot's note is to center in the name Tiresias. For his part, Eliot can measure Pound's comments and know when to listen to him and when to ignore him, and those instances where he ignores Pound are as telling as the others.

Eliot's ear for mimicry was not always true. In "The Game of Chess" (originally "In the Cage," a title tying the section closer to the epigraph from Petronius he eventually used), Eliot writes, "When Lil's husband was coming back out of the Transport Corps." Then he tries, "Discharged out of the army?" Pound writes firmly "demobbed," which stands. At a different level of diction, Mr. Eugenide's "abominable" French becomes "demotic" at Pound's hand. The anachronistic "closed carriage" ("Why this Blot on Scutchen/between 1922 and Lil") becomes "closed car."[1]   When Eliot allows Tiresias to speculate about what goes on in the typist's head in a line reading "Across her brain one half-formed thought may pass," Pound scolds in the margin: "make up yr. mind/you Tiresias/if you know/know damn well or else you don't." This longest section of the published poem originally shifted to quatrains with the line introducing Tiresias, "At the violet hour." There are numerous pencil marks in Pound's hand here, till he reaches the point of exasperation where he declares "*verse* not interesting enough as verse to warrant so much of it." In the other margin he twits Eliot "*qui dira les gaffers de la rime*," adapting a sentence from Verlaine. He quarrels with inversions, with phrases too easy, such as "crawling bugs." Pound is manifestly right about such details. And the quatrian is wrong as well. Eliot can use the quatrain for dry or caustic irony with great compression, as in the Sweeney poems. But in the interest of unresolved pathos, for a sense of loss in which that which is lost is not yet clearly seen and named, a higher strain serves him better, as in the opening lines of "The Game of Chess." Eliot had begun the section of his poem he calls "The Fire Sermon" with a long series of couplets after the manner and matter of Pope's *Rape of the Lock,* in which he presents a modern Belinda named Fresca. Here Pound notes again that "rhyme drags it out to diffuseness"; again, "trick of Pope etc. not to let couple[t] diffuse 'em." Eliot discards the seventy-odd lines, since Pound convinces him Pope did that bit better. It is an imitation, and the inappropriateness of

Eliot's light satiric run is in sharp contrast to the scene which also echoes Pope, but at a darker level and not in Pope's style: the first half of "The Game of Chess" introduces the deadly lady at her looking glass, trapped and entrapping in a fatal ennui.

Eliot reduces the Tiresias quatrains from sixty-eight lines down to thirty-four, in which we have now only a residual rhyme, hauntingly effective in spite of their accidental discovery. But he is less disturbed than Pound about the first twenty-five lines of "The Game of Chess" that are "Too tumpum at a stretch" and beside which Vivien has written, "Don't see what you had in mind here." What Eliot seems to have in mind, or at least the effect those lines manage, is of an exquisite though momentary recovery of dead art and history, vividly present in a sensual, musical language which Keats might envy. The decayed pageantry, fleetingly sustained by the flickering imagination, is suddenly collapsed with "And still she cried and still the world pursues,/'Jug Jug' to dirty ears." The Keatsean play of *still* is as destructive of the suspension of the lover's bower by the imagination as the sudden intrusion of *forlorn* that makes certain fancy is but deceiving elf. What one is left with is a residue, the "withered stumps of time," in the light of which decay (compare the "sunlight on broken columns" of *The Hollow Men*) the drama of love's emptiness is played out in a monotonous colloquy between the lady before her mirror and the empty, sardonic man who waits the completion of her toilet.[2]

In Part IV, the "Death by Water" section of the manuscript, Pound persuades Eliot to discard three "bad" quatrains that introduce a long monologue written too much in the manner of Tennyson's "Ulysses." There is an awkwardly quoted phrase from Tennyson's poem ("much seen and much endured") which in context is embarrassing. Eliot discards the quatrains and, reluctantly, the seventy-one lines of monologue. That he was partial to them and hesitant to discard them in reason enough to look more closely at them. Though initially Tennysonian in material and manner, the monologue moves toward an ending which echoes the situation of the "Rhyme of the Ancient Mariner." Because he is still hopeful of them, Eliot submits a revised version to Pound, in a very long section including the lines now constituting "Death by Water." Included as well were the lines that now stand (after minor corrections and revisions) as the final

section, "What the Thunder Said." After Pound's promised
"attack" on the new version, which leaves only the ten lines
standing in the IV section, Eliot wonders whether they too may
not be discarded. Pound responds, "I DO advise keeping Phlebas.
In fact I more'n advise. Phlebas is an integral part of the poem;
the card pack introduces him, the drowned phoen. sailor. And
he is needed ABSOLOOTLY where he is. Must stay in."

What is to be debated in this drastic cutting of ninety-two
lines down to ten is not the discarding of the weak quatrains
but the exclusion of Eliot's "Ulysses" monologue. I take it that
Pound is right to urge their exclusion, though not for his reasons
we deduce from his notes and letters to Eliot. We notice at
once about the lines that they are full of Eliot's experiences with
sailing on the New England coast, but the pleasure of the personal recollection prevents the misery and terror of ill fortune,
which is introduced near the end, from ringing true. By the end
of the passage, the experience which the lines are intended to
convey has largely disappeared and become merely a telling—a
counting—of points in narrative in which neither the tone, nor
the narrative events imagined beyond the personal recollection
of sailing, are convincing at a narrative or dramatic level.

And yet one can see very well from the passage why Eliot
is interested in them, as well as why he is drawn to Conrad, who
provides a discarded epigraph to the whole poem. He has recognized in myth and metaphor a narrative potential which might
point to a dramatic center. He is drawn to the sea journey as a
term to relate an intellectual struggle whose issue must be a
movement, a turning of the mind. In the discarded lines the tension is relieved by a narrative detail less understatement than
bathos, "Then came the fish at last. . ." That narrative step
enters upon terror, the hallucination of three women singing in
the fore cross-trees, leaving the narrator at a cocktail party to
recover from the experience. ("Where's a cocktail shaker, Ben,
here's plenty of ice.") The material and its presentation are not
commensurate to the experience in which he is "frightened beyond fear, horrified past horror, calm." The surrealistic terror
in "What the Thunder Said" shows by contrast that Eliot fails
the fusion necessary, such a fusion as Conrad manages through
the quiet approach to horror by Marlow. Eliot attempts to come
at last to the shattering experience in those nether regions Dante
and Tennyson imitate with the last voyage of Odysseus and

Conrad with Kurtz's inland jouney to the heart of darkness. It is at this point in the manuscript that the enigmatic lines of the drowned New England and Phoenician sailor "a fortnight dead" occur. We might guess here that Eliot is concerned with the inadequacy of the modern world's paganism, particularly the pragmatic New England version of it that he was struggling to divest himself of. His mind is to deal more explicitly with the problem in *The Idea of a Christian Society* (1940), but that prose adumbration of the problem is foreshadowed in the Phleas lines in the faint echo of St. Paul's "Gentile or Jew."[3] As the lines stand in the public version of *The Waste Land*, they indeed mark a turning point essential to that unity Pound sees encompassed from *April* to *shantih*. For the introduction of Paul marks the beginning of the new direction Eliot takes that separates him more and more from Pound.

Before considering the distinction suggested between narrative and dramatic action in the reading of Eliot's discarded monologue, and the effect upon the question of the poem's unity and the problem of its point of view in such a destruction, we may notice a problem Pound seems more acutely aware of than Eliot as a threat to Eliot's success in the poem. It is a danger Eliot came to see in retrospect, one may imagine, as in his comment on "In Memoriam" (1936). There, contrasting Tennyson's narrative gift to Dante's, he remarks that "Dante is telling a story. Tennyson is only stating an elegiac mood." It is the *stated* elegiac mood, with a looseness and flabbiness out of the nineteenth century, that bothers Pound about the monologue; his penciled remarks indicate that concern. But it is the *unity* of Eliot's narrative—with its beginning, middle, but (above all) too much a statement of an ending—that works against the feel of the material as a whole. The lines were wisely discarded by Eliot, in spite of his feeling for them. They were not abandoned. They are subsequently assimilated in a new richness made possible by the struggle which *The Waste Land* represents and which issues in "Ash-Wednesday" upon that mountain Dante's Ulysses could not win. The essential burden of the lines on the New England Phoenician sailor reappear as a more impressive part of Eliot's poetry in *Dry Salvages.*

NOTES

[1]A point overlooked by the *Times Literary Supplement* reviewer of the manuscript edition, who says ". . .this question Eliot ignores. A specific locality and a particular date were the last things he was concerned with." (December 10, 1971) A considerable over-simplification in the light of the demon history Eliot wrestles in the poem, in addition to being a misreading of the text.

[2]Simultaneously, Aldous Huxley is presenting a version of this region of *The Waste Land* in *Chrome Yellow* (1921) and *Antic Hay* (1923). In *Antic Hay* Lady Viveash stands in the final scene with the comic hollow man, Theodore Gumbril Junior, looking out across the Thames ("across the flow of time") to St. Paul's, which floats "up as though self-supported in the moonlight." Behind them Shearwater on a stationary bicycle is "pedalling unceasingly like a man in a nightmare" the object of an experiment in exhaustion. A cage of rats "fed on milk from a London dairy" are getting thinner each day, except for one fed Grade A from the country: it is so fat it can hardly move. Lady Viveash with her empty eyes on St. Paul's breathes "expiringly from her death-bed within" the final truth of the London world the novel maintains: "To-morrow. . .will be as awful as to-day." Huxley's comic mode, as in the impish audacity of his character names and their situations, rather highlights the accidie of the hour.

[3]In *The Idea of a Christian Society*, Eliot predicts a "totalitarian democracy" which will have much in common with other pagan societies." It will dictate a "puritanism of hygienic morality in the interest of efficiency; uniformity of opinion through propaganda, and art only encouraged when it flutters the official doctrines of the time." (pp. 21-22) We must respect Eliot as seer as we observe toothpaste and deodorant ads on television or the pitch made for art as "relevant" from the popular book reviews of current fiction to the plethora of texts for freshman composition courses built on what is "in" at the moment with the freshman mind. The revolt against this form of paganism in their elders by our recent unwashed youth, with their attempt to shock sensibilities through more blatant pagan antics, is implicit in Eliot's remark (in "Thoughts after Lambeth," 1931)

that "youth, of course, is from one point of view merely a symptom of the results of what the middle-aged have been thinking and saying." Already about them there are the signs of "a new respectability" which will accept only the present; it is a force, the burden of which came to bear upon our universities in the late 1960s. Eliot describes that force's agents: ". . .those who would once have been considered intellectual vagrants are now pious pilgrims, cheerfully plodding the road from nowhere to nowhere, trolling their hymns, satisfied as long as they may be 'on the march'." The characterization applies no less to the administrative powers of the multiversities, those nightmares of the unanchored mind, than to homeless youth movements.

IV

UNDISCIPLINED SQUADS OF EMOTION

In the general mess of imprecision of feeling,
Undisciplined squads of emotion.

East Coker

There is a unity in *The Waste Land*. But in order to see the nature of it we must penetrate the narrative surface to reach a dramatic center, for if we dwell to long upon the surface, we must agree with Conrad Aiken's early summary (*New Republic*, February 7, 1923):

> I think. . .that the poem must be taken. . .as a brilliant and kaleidoscopic confusion; as a series of sharp, discrete, slightly related perceptions and feelings, dramatically and lyrically presented, and violently juxtaposed (for effect or dissonance), so as to give us an impression of an intensely modern, intensely literary consciousness which perceives itself to be not a unit but a chance correlation or conglomerate of mutually discolorative fragments.

That is a richly rewarding approach to Eliot's poem, but we must go deeper, being finally unsatisfied by Aiken's conclusion that "the poem succeeds. . .by virtue of its incoherence, not of its plan; by virtue of its ambiguities, not of its explanations." Nor are many readers content to accept the poem as they would "accept a powerful, melancholy tone-poem," as Aiken finally advises us to do. To do so leaves unaccounted for that nagging quality of the poem, that feeling that we are in the presence of a crucial encounter in which life itself is changed. We require an aesthetic justification, which Aiken's commentary seems adequate to provide, but then we find ourselves requiring a justification other than, or beyond, the aesthetic, or else we are reduced finally—with the passage of time—to that poem as historical document, to the conclusion that it represents that lost generation of "an intensely modern, intensely literary consciousness which perceives itself to be not a unit but a chance correlation or conglomerate of mutually discolorative fragments." That is to say, we expect more of those fragments shored against our ruin than merely an artistic representation of a sensitive and confused mind anchored in a point of time. And our very expectation itself is a clue to the dramatic center of the poem.

The difficulty of discovering a principle of exclusion troubles Eliot greatly as he attempts to bring form to his fragments, as we have seen in his struggle to justify his "Ulysses" fragment. Somewhere between the deadly rigidity of an idea forcing order and the chaos of automatic writing lies a balance which allows imaginative impulse or vision an accommodation to conscious artistry. Joyce's mastery of the stream of consciousness, which so convincingly demonstrated the old maxim that art hides art, highlights the possibility. In Donne and the Metaphysicals Eliot sees a similar effective balance. It is the pursuit of an accommodation of thought's force to thought's form which leads Eliot to discuss the problem of language under famous (or infamous) namings of the problem such as "objective correlative" and the "dissociation of sensibility."[1]

Eliot has wrestled the problem no less in his poetry than in his essays. In "Whispers of Immortality" we have already been given a wry, self-deprecating comment on the inability of the finest poetic minds to unite the metaphysical and physical in words. There is an implication of inadequacy in Webster and Donne, as if to say the dissociation of sensibility has roots further back in English poetry than the interval of Dryden and Milton. The Metaphysical, too, fails to express the essential soul which our desire—our expectation—will not abandon, that soul that whispers below or beyond the poet's word, circumambulating even Grishkin's worldliness. One can, with such sophistication, perceive the mortality in flesh, grading from the obvious to the less obvious, from the immediate to the metaphorical. From a fleshly Grishkin to marmoset, with both *words* and *jaguar* devouring to the bones, but not able to expose or destroy the marrow in our bones: that promise (expectation) that they shall rise again.

It is interesting in this connection to read Brice Parain's *A Metaphysics of Language,* which argues language as jaguar. He remarks, for instance, that words are always at war with existence. "Nightingales have no need of poets; each of them is a poet, superbly, fittingly and with simplicity." Again, "Language is fertile only because it devours existence." And again, "Why not. . .invert *cogito* and say: I think therefore I am not. For to think is not be be, it is to wish to be." And a final word from Parain: "Speech, because it is made to communicate with others, consequently to share in what we have in common, can only

accommodate the impersonal part of each [with any assurance]
. . . Hence the present conflict between obscure poetry, the
child of freedom, and the vocation of language, the province of
philosophy." The poet, in Parain's evaluation, is eternally
doomed to failure, since what he pursues—Eliot's still point,
Wordsworth's spots of time, a state of being at one with the self
and the All—is impossible of realization to him as poet because
words rare irreconcilably destructive of the goal pursued. Eliot's
interest in Rimbaud is largely a fascination with the silence
that Rimbaud's pursuit of freedom brings him to. Parain, pursuing the irreconcilable dilemma between *words* and *being*, asserts a solution finally by cutting the Gordian knot. "Logically,
language can no more be a basis for itself than thought can think
itself. We should not be overastonished when metaphysics
sooner or later destroys itself, as happened in Greece after
Socrates, and nearer to our time with Kant. There remains then
the Prince, he who simply asserts that language is the means of
the mind which reveals itself thus, and so exercises its sovereignty. But this affirmation to be clearly what it must be cannot be
simply a proposition. It has to be an act. . ." It is a resolution
of the problem of language that Pound comes to very early; he
acts out his poetry with the consequent risks, though one of
those risks is not, as it must be with the reflective poet such as
Eliot, the threat of silence.

As for Eliot, the best he can manage with Grishkin is that
she is *nice,* understatement as a comment on the failure of
words to reveal to another mind the whisper beneath the whisper
of the flesh. Our lot crawls between dry ribs to keep our metaphysics warm, Eliot says of the word's inadequacies, going on to
indict himself more particularly in "Mr. Eliot's Sunday Morning
Service," though protecting himself as is usual before the time of
"Gerontion" with the shield of irony. It is not until Eliot has
entered into the mind of Bishop Andrewes that he can discover
an acceptable justification of words. In that essay on Andrewes
(1926) he takes issue with Donne, and by implication with his
own earlier (1919) faith in the "objective correlative." In
Andrewes' sermons he discovers the problem of the word set
more largely than in the context of philosophical phenomenology, the pursuit of being through unaided reason, or of an aesthetic built on the imaginative detail. The proper setting for the
problem of language is now in the Word, so that language's inadequacies can be accepted and language itself justified. In

other words, Eliot has begun to move more freely into the desert
land of paradox from the safe cold heights of irony. In doing
so, he sets Donne beneath Andrewes: "Donne is constantly
finding an object which shall be adequate to his feelings; Andrewes is wholly absorbed in the object and therefore responds
with the adequate emotion." To seek the object to fit the feeling is to be impure, and so Eliot remarks that "about Donne
there hangs the shadow of the impure motive; and impure motives lend their aid to a facile success." His evidence for the
evaluation is not poetry but the sermons of each man; yet one
can hardly escape the realization that Eliot's judgment is reflecting upon his own poetry. In the comments of his essay lies part
of the explication of those lines he subsequently writes in which
he asserts that at the still point of the turning world (and the
poet's word), one discovers that "the poetry does not matter/It
was not (to start again) what one had expected." Eliot then
is to reach a point where poetry and philosophy, ideas and their
dramatically resonant music, seem reconcilable, a point from
which he will evaluate both poetry and philosophy in a different
plane.[2]

At the time of *The Waste Land*, Eliot has no such position,
and because Pound is so decisively bold where questions of
aesthetics are concerned, Eliot places his trust in Pound and
is persuaded to reject from the poem sections to which he feels
an intimate attraction beyond their literary merit, or beyond
what Pound declares to be their literary merit. We may enlarge
somewhat upon Eliot's difficulty, though one must proceed more
cautiously than the reviewer of the manuscript for the *Times
Literary Supplement*.   That reviewer is rather insistent that
Eliot's imagination is Virgilian rather than Homeric (*TLS*, December 10, 1971).   Pound, he contends, mistook the point, in
consequence of which his influence anchors our public version
of *The Waste Land* in London life more overtly than had been
Eliot's intention in writing it. He cites the beginning lines of the
first version of "The Burial of the Dead" which present a Boston
salon milieu, roughly paralleling the London pub scene of the
present "Game of Chess."

What we might say about the reviewer's point, to make it
more accurate, is that Eliot at the moment had not so much a
Virgilian imagination as a Virgilian awareness: an enormous
suspension of fragments from history and art, present and past,

which lacked that very quality of intellect in Virgil through which the Roman poet could bring his intellect and imagination into a complementary focus. That is, Eliot lacked a cause, a principle, to which he could give consent. To put the point another way, Eliot had a Virgilian mind seeking its Virgil, and in an irony of literary history which inverted an old relationship, he discovered Dante to be his true Virgil. Eliot's is a consciousness, at this point of his own journey, too personally involved with the momentary *act* of discovery to exercise the control necessary to a finished work of art of the scale he undertook. Pound takes too simply the real crisis in Eliot when he considers his difficulties a nervous breakdown, brought about by overwork in Lloyd's and the personal complication of Vivien's health. That simplification nevertheless made it possible for Pound to act, as Eliot could not, and with the manuscript as an object for action both Pound and Eliot could be distracted from the deeper crisis Eliot was experiencing. It was a crisis whose issue Pound could have little sympathy with, an issue which will lead Pound later to speak disparagingly of "Parson Eliot."

   With Pound's help, Eliot discovers a form for his long poem, a joint process quite different from that imaginative act of the *Four Quartets,* which, turning back upon *The Waste Land* experience, establishes in each of the quartets a structure and movement refining and paralleling the more famous poem.[3]   Indeed, our *TLS* reviewer is very wide of the mark when he asserts that the manuscript makes it "quite clear that Eliot at no time was concerned to register the 'out there' of London life at a specific epoch.' " It is precisely what Eliot is trying to do. To register the *out there* in words, and through them bring self-awareness to an accommodation with all that is not the self—this has been the struggle in Eliot's poetry from the beginning and it is the struggle he will continue.

   He is not, of course, writing history or philosophy; nor is he acting out the role of the poet in society as Pound thought necessary. That is why he will assert later, in "Thoughts after Lambeth" (1931): "I dislike the word 'generation'. When I wrote a poem called *The Waste Land* some of the more approving critics said that I had expressed 'the disillusionment of a generation,' which is nonsense. I may have expressed for them their own illusion of being disillusioned, but that did not form a part of my intention." What one must remember in reading that statement is that Eliot is writing specifically as a Christian; whereas Virgil's imagination finds its focus in the service of social unity, Eliot's (and Dante's) asserts that the individual soul must contend with its own "illusion of being disillusioned," from which it can make no significant escape into the protective generality of such terms as generation or society or the age.

Eliot's assertion then by no means justifies our concluding that he had no interest in the "out there." Up to the time of *The Waste Land,* he has hardly had any other intellectual in-terest, since his most pressing problem has been to ratify his own consciousness, which he can do only through the "out there," the Other which is not the Self. It is a deliberate choice on his part to study Bradley's philosophy for his dissertation, and the consuming problem of that study is to reconcile consciousness to that which it is conscious of. The search for the key to that problem is under way from the beginning, nowhere more vividly present than in his "Preludes" and "Rhapsody on a Windy Night," but present also in those *Poems Written in Early Youth.*

In *Poems Written in Early Youth* one notices the romantic pose of emptiness and separation, which undergoes ironic refine-ment as the influence of Jules Laforgue becomes a part of them. If there is initially a greater concern with being a poet—the most usual early stage—and consequently less intensity than will occur as the young poet is set adrift by the pose, there are nevertheless the ideas and questions present that will presently become over-whelming. Thus when we see that "life, a little bald and gray,/ Languid, fastidious and bland/Waits. . ./On the doorstep of the Absolute," we are not arrested as we shall be by that "Eternal Footman" who holds Prufrock's coat and snickers. There is the "fragrance of bloom and fragrance of decay" in those flowers of "Before Morning," a problem whose intensity lies ahead through lilacs and hyacinths and roses, a problem to be settled in a garden by a lady going in Mary's colors. That lady in "On a Portrait" stands "beyond the circle of our thoughts," teasing-ly, without the disturbing influence of the lady of the portrait immediately ahead in Eliot's first volume. And Saint Narcissus is a Tiresias, having been tree, fish, young girl, with the agony of metamorphic thoughts, becoming a "dancer to God/Because his flesh was in love with the burning arrows." With "Nocturne," dedicated to Laforgue, we come upon a narrator pleased by the world sustained by a thought "in my best mode oblique," through which mode Eliot will more seriously engage the themes and ideas implicit from the beginning; that is, engage them out the corner of his eye, a slant increasingly unbearable until he must turn with direct eyes to the problem of the Self and the Other in "Ash-Wednesday," having promised to meet us directly and openly on such questions in "Gerontion."

We are not safe in supposing that the footnotes he chose to append to *The Waste Land* are to be rejected out of hand because the mellow Eliot characterizes them as a "remarkable exposition of bogus scholarship" which "stimulated the wrong kind of interest among seekers of sources." ("The Frontiers of Criticism," *Sewanee Review*, Autumn 1956) If the citation of Chapman's *Handbook of Birds of Eastern North America*, and the quotation from it to identify the hermit thrush, have about them something of the leg pull, it might make us dwell upon that creature long enough to recall a relation to Whitman. We may see that those lines from "What the Thunder Said" (lines 350-359) represent a subtle break with Walt Whitman and his world as we compare them to Whitman's own account of a vision in Section 15 of "When Lilacs Last in the Dooryard Bloomed." And we may return from the "wild goose chase after Tarot cards and the Holy Grail" which the reference to Jessie Weston's book sent us on to consider whether there is not more dissatisfaction than approval of her understanding of the quest in his use of her materials.

But there are two notes of extreme importance to the problem of the poem's unity and significance, the one seemingly of a technical nature, the other seemingly of a philosophical, which we must not discard. Tiresias, we are told, "although a mere spectator and not indeed a 'character,' is yet the most important personage in the poem, uniting all the rest." It is a clue to reading the poem, but it is much more. The second is a passage quoted from F. H. Bradley's *Appearance and Reality*, as subordinate to the primary analogue Eliot points to in Dante's *Purgatorio*.

Eliot consistently asserts his gratitude to Bradley to the end of his days; but not because Bradley gave satisfactory answer to the problem of the Self and the Other. It is rather because Bradley taught him to take the problem of romanticism seriously: the sense of loss, separation, emptiness, hunger for a center of

rest. And Bradley did so with a humility one does not always encounter in the philosopher. Eliot remembers, for instance, that
Bradley defines metaphysics as "the finding of bad reasons for
what we believe upon instinct, but to find those reasons is no
less an instinct." Through Bradley, Eliot learns to put the uses
of philosophy in a perspective; *what* that perspective is to be he
discovers in Augustine, Paul, Pascal. *How* to focus his sight in
words—in poems—he learns from Laforgue, Donne, Baudelaire,
but most importantly from Dante.

The passage from Bradley which Eliot quotes in his footnote contains the idea necessary to our discovery of the dramatic
center of the poem and to our seeing that Tiresias does more
than suggest a solution to the problem of the technical point of
view. Eliot's quotation from Bradley reads:

> My external sensations are no less private to myself than
> are my thoughts or my feelings. In either case my ex-
> perience falls within my own circle, a circle closed on the
> outside; and, with all its elements alike, every sphere is
> opaque to the others which surround it. . . In brief, re-
> garded as an existence which appears a soul, the whole
> world for each is peculiar and private to that soul.

If Bradley is right, then the passage can hardly be one of en-
couragement to the restless, alienated modern; for what it asserts is that alienation allows no solution. We must be forever
limited by the impossibility of getting "beyond the circle of our
thoughts." The point is not that Bradley asserts a final conclusion of the problem's inconclusiveness, any more than Jessie
Weston's argument of the procreative level of the grail quest is
the complete revelation (through Freud's help) of the quest.
The passage is cited by Eliot in relation to lines in the poem
that declare a key to have been found to unlock the door of the
self, to unclose the circle. The key which has turned once,
locking the little world of what "appears a soul," is self-awareness. The agony of Eliot's lines from his first volume up to the
fifth section of *The Waste Land* carries evidence of an attempt
to ratify intimations of a world separate from the self, on evidence of an "out there" filtered through the senses into the consciousness. It is a struggle whose solution will presently prove
acceptable to Eliot in an understanding beyond reason, the
paradoxical center of which he has already introduced in that

oblique of himself named Gerontion: "The word within a word, unable to speak a work." Up to *The Waste Land* he has wrestled with the word of the finite mind as the key, admitting a defeat in the "Preludes," in "Whispers of Immortality," in "Gerontion." It is the poem "Gerontion" which Eliot suggests as an appropriate preface to *The Waste Land.* (Pound responds, "I advise you NOT to print "Gerontion" as prelude.")

With his poetry behind him, Eliot comments in an interview with Donald Hall for the *Paris Review,* on the evolution of his poems and fragments of poems into larger wholes: "That's one way in which my mind does seem to have worked through the years—doing things separately and then seeing the possibility of fusing them together, altering them, and making a kind of whole of them." The history of the "Preludes," "The Hollow Men," and "Ash-Wednesday," the incorporation of "Saint Narcissus" or "Dans le Restaurant" into *The Waste Land* manuscript are evidence of such workings of his mind. But once more it is not simply a matter of craftsmanship—of revision. Eliot's is the reflective mind at work, and in reflection it grows to contain itself as it examines itself. For that reason an examination of his first two volumes leads to a highlighting of "Prufrock" in the one and "Gerontion" in the other as poems central to the thought of each volume. The title of the first volume subordinates the "Other Observations." The title of the English edition of the second volume *Ara Vos Prec* ("Now I pray you," from *Purgatory,* XXVI) calls us to be mindful most particularly of Gerontion's pain.

When he can come to terms with the Word, Eliot will be ready to re-enter the community of the lost generation, but it will be the generation of Adam and not that of the 1920s. And when he does return from that journey begun under the auspices of Saint Narcissus with news for the world outside—that he is classicist, royalist, Anglo-Catholic—it will be to find himself considered naive or reactionary or traitorous by those once comfortable with him—Pound, Aiken, William Carlos Williams, his old friend and teacher Irving Babbitt. Before that return, however, there is the problem with the "out there" which he must solve.

NOTES

[1]Though Eliot intends a preciseness to "feeling" as a counter to Wordsworth's "emotion," his handling of the term has not proved helpful under close examination. See Elesio Vivas's "The Objective Correlative of T. S. Eliot," *Creation and Discovery,* for instance. Jacques Maritain (whom Eliot translated early in the *Criterion* and thought highly of) sets his opposition to the term more persuasively in a metaphysical context congenial to Eliot's concern. See pages 106 through 145 of *Creative Intuition in Art and Poetry* (1953), handily available in *Challenges and Renewals: Selected Readings,* edited by Joseph W. Evans and Leo R. Ward, Meridian Book 252.

[2]That eventual position makes hauntingly pathetic the letter Eliot's mother writes Bertrand Russell in 1916, in which she separates the callings. New England Puritan to her bones, yet consumed with the poet's fire herself, she pleads with Russell: "I am sure your influence in every way will confirm my son in his choice of Philosophy as a life rock. . . I had hoped he would seek a University appointment next year. If he does not I shall feel regret. I have absolute faith in his Philosophy but not in the vers libres." (The letter is quoted by Russell in Volume II of his *Autobiography.*) Eliot's refusal to abandon poetry found a sterner rebuke at the hands of his father, whose will effectively cut off Eliot's inheritance because of his residence in England and his seemingly wasteful life as poet. Russell's "influence in every way" had included, earlier that year (in January 1916), his taking Vivien Eliot to Torquay for a holiday while Eliot remained in London. On first meeting her, Russell had discovered Vivien to be "light, a little vulgar, adventurous, full of life." (An evaluation of her shared by Aldoux Huxley, who speaks of her in 1918 as a "genuine person, vulgar, but with no attempt to conceal her vulgarity.") The holiday, considered in the context of Russell's recollections, seems obviously a private sensitivity treatment beyond the reaches of propriety, but Eliot's thank-you note (which Russell publishes for us) seems to lack all traces of irony: "Dear Bertie: This is wonderfully kind of you—really the last straw (so to speak) of generosity. I am very sorry you have come back—and Vivien says you have been an angel to her. . . I am sure you have done *everything* [Eliot's italics] possible and handled her in the very best way. . . I believe

we shall owe her life to you, even."

3 *The Waste Land* is rivaled by the *Four Quartets* at this juncture of Eliot criticism. The question of whether they are one poem or four, whether within each of the four the parts can be reconciled, occupies attention, and the heart of the debate is set forth by Donald Davie in his defense of *The Dry Salvages,* which "sticks out among the rest like a sore thumb," on the grounds that it is simply *rather a bad poem."* Building on Hugh Kenner's "Eliot's Moral Dialectic" (*Hudson Review,* 1949), Davie argues that *Dry Salvages* is deliberate self-parody, a false resolution of opposites penultimate to their true reconciliation in *Little Gidding.* See "T. S. Eliot: The End of an Era," *The Twentieth Century,* CLIX, No. 950, reprinted in *T. S. Eliot: A Collection of Critical Essays,* edited by Hugh Kenner for Prentice-Hall, Inc., 1962.

V

MEMORY AND DESIRE:
THE "PRELUDES" AS PRELUDE

> Not the intense moment
> Isolated, with no before and after,
> But a lifetime burning in every moment.

East Coker

The problem of reconciling consciousness and its objects is complicated by those aspects of consciousness announced in the opening lines of the public *Waste Land: memory* and *desire.* Memory is unverifiable. Eliot's old teacher Bertrand Russell puts the problem: one cannot distinguish memory images from pure imagination, i.e., willed illusion. How can one place any reasoned confidence in that "feeling of pastness" which suggests that there is a difference between the present moment of awareness and past moments of awareness? To suggest that a complete world created one moment before the present, containing all memory and knowledge, is beyond proof may be "uninteresting" to Russell, beyond posing the problem as insoluble, though his *Autobiography* suggests his confidence in the pastness of the past and its real existence. But it cannot be so to Eliot. Eliot is attracted to Russell initially, and learns much from him at the outset, but he cannot stand on the same ground, as he rapidly discovers. He cannot, because his *desire* is such as to disallow a focus upon the instrument of the mind, the logical structures the mind makes, as Russell can comfortably do. Eliot must come to terms with the maker of such instruments, the mind itself. The "Preludes" is the first significant dramatization of this struggle which is to rise to a climax in the final section of *The Waste Land,* at a point where we may bring Tiresias into conjunction with the key which releases Eliot from the necessity of that literary device of point of view and from an entrapment in the Bradleyan dilemma of thought's relation to its object.

If memory is difficult of verification, desire seems inexplicable. Hence the vague restlessness in that carefully controlled sequence of the "Preludes," a sequence of poems composed over a period of four years, in America and France, coming to only fifty-four lines. In the first section *evening* is a collective for the images of its thirteen lines, which in their movement, metrics, and rhyme suggest a compressed Shakespearean sonnet. The time is present, and if there is a past for memory to reflect upon, it is indistinguishable from the present. Indeed time present, time past and time future are emptily included in the singular "six o'clock." That verse which effectively rests a time interval approximating that of the tetrameter verse which is the basic measure of Section I. Empty timelessness (the condition opposite that of the still point we shall come to) is suspended in the descriptive extension of the third line, which completes the first quatrain: "The burnt-out ends of smoky days." There is an illusion of action in the next eight lines, random and inconsequential, with a suggestion of conclusion in the last line, set off by space from the preceding ones, yet yoked by couplet rhyme (*stamps-lamps*). But there is hardly conclusion in "And then the lighting of the lamps;" the light available is at best one to the senses, the established tone emphasizing the futility of such light to dispel the settling darkness. The darkness is hardly remarkable enough to warrant metaphorical tags such as Shakespeare conjures from similar images: death's second self, for instance. The isolation of this "entity," this awareness, from the "out there" is signalled in the adjectives that attach to attempts to name the outer world, and we may reflect how far removed the gusty shower of "Preludes" is from the hint of rain in the final section of *The Waste Land*. Nor is there much of a suggestion of judgment in the adjectives attached to nouns in the "Preludes" as there is in the description of the Thames in *The Waste Land*. We have rather a despondent acknowledgment of isolation: *withered* leaves; *vacant* lots; *broken* blinds and chimney pots; even the cab-horse is, hopefully, lonely. To simply name the objects of that other world is a species of pathetic fallacy, requiring no metaphor or personification.

One need only compare analogous phrases from another "romantic" poem to see the oppressiveness of the closed world the mind of "Preludes" contends with. In the first paragraph of Wordsworth's "Tintern Abbey," a reflective awareness is opening upon a larger world with increasing confidence, through "steep and lofty cliffs," from under its own "dark sycamore." In the midst of a "deep secluded" wood there is notice, even if uncertain, of a larger life of the mind which the mind alone must take credit for in Eliot's poem. Wordsworth, in his poem, is recording a coming to himself in a dark wood, that darkness lying in the mind. One sees him accepting metaphor as more than device, through a coincidence too particularly appropriate to be coincidence. At high noon, at midyear, midway a river on its way to the sea, he reflects upon his own point midway life, as Dante has done before him; and he certifies metaphor as more valid than a quaint device of words, being persuaded by the correspondences between the moment in his mind and the moment of nature's world that his senses certify to him.

Wordsworth comes to a new consciousness, but in Eliot's poem only *morning* comes to consciousness, *morning* itself a weak collective like *evening.* The *morning* collects, through images, an additional assertion of separation of each of Bradley's "closed circles," the small world of each consciousness which is peculiar and private and so capable of being registered only as masquerades such as will be more fully displayed by Prufrock. Indeed *morning, evening* name a mask for the entity or awareness of Eliot's poem. Nor will Keats's negative capability serve as a key to unlock the private world upon the Other. To assert that *"your* soul" is constituted of a "thousand sordid images" flickering against the ceiling only certifies *"my* soul," the realization of which calls up the sardonic tone at the end of Eliot's poem. To hear the "sparrows in the gutters" is not to enter that world of the *you,* futilely addressed in the third section of the poem. How forlorn the prospect of shouting with Achilles in the trenches. Neither the *street* (another collective substitute for the closed world of the poem's awareness, as *evening* and *morning* have been) nor the *you* share a common "vision." At best the *you* is a metaphorical projection of the self upon that object clasping yellow soles of feet in soiled hands—and we are prepared through this section for the first line of Prufrock by this realization. Neither *street* nor *you* shares a vision with the speaking voice; neither Wordsworth's Nature nor his Dorothy can signify community larger than the self in Eliot's poem. The speaking voice then can only enunciate additional images which float hollowly in its own locked world. The mind as a mansion for all lovely forms, the memory as a dwelling place for all sweet sounds and harmonies, has become a ghostly horror house through which awareness drags its sad weight.

And yet that is not quite all. There is a *desire* which will not be stilled. There are eyes that seem assured of certain certainties, even if they will not or cannot reflect them clearly to reveal vision such as Dorothy's eyes do to Wordsworth on the banks of the Wye or Beatrice's to Dante on the shores of Lethe.[1] The conscience of this blackened street, and the consciousness that inhabits the "Preludes," is impatient to assume the world. There is a momentary movement as if the key is about to be turned in the lock. Then fear-haunted desire succumbs to fear. The certainty of illusion is the only certainty, where desire is but fancy. The poem concludes that, through fancy, the desire only "curls" around images and "clings" to them. The joyful declaration of a Wordsworth that something is deeply interfused in nature, resident of setting suns, round oceans, and the mind of man through the forms that inhabit his mind—the confidence that there is a larger and more inclusive existence than individual awareness—is not to be trusted. Wordsworth can hear the "still, sad music of humanity," with its powers to chasten and subdue the consciousness, because of his sense of a presence which he accepts as valid perception; *desire* is to Wordsworth a valid spring in the opening of the door of the separate self. But in the "Preludes," there is only

> The *notion* of some infinitely gentle
> Infinitely suffering thing.

That *thing* seems at best the awareness in its own locked world, in which the poem is suspended. Lacking the daring risk of a surrender to illusion, it must recover its poise, laugh sardonically, wiping a hand across the mouth. The *your* of the line third from last is most private, hardly turned out toward the reader as we shall find that word doing in "Gerontion." It declares those worlds, which Donne and Shakespeare found cunningly contrived of angelic sprite and earth, to be merely revolving, each on its axis, each a peculiar and private world incapable of constellation.

If that were all that one might conclude, if the "argument" implied by the "Preludes" were one subscribed to completely by Eliot, the poem must needs be his last. After this, silence, as in Rimbaud, whom Eliot finds fascinating till he comes to that larger silence and stillness such as might be represented by St. Thomas Aquinas's closing his book and writing no more. What Eliot cannot escape, and what therefore keeps desire alive as it did in Wordsworth, is the haunting presence of what Husserl calls "Original Intuition." That the poem exists at all is an evidence of that intuition and a contradiction of the poem's fears. It is the same intuition that will not let a Coleridge rest in the pure mechanics of mind out of David Hartley, or Wordsworth find peace in the solipsism of Bishop Berkeley. For, as the "Preludes" attempts to dramatize, consciousness is of *something*; it cannot exist without some self-evident something of which it cannot be concluded the first cause; nor can it conclude that the coming to rest of that something in the consciousness, the settling of dregs in sterile water, is the final cause. Self-awareness cannot exist unless it is at least aware of itself, a point resurrected by Husserl and dwelt upon subsequently by Bradley and Whitehead. (The point is as ancient as Augustine, in whom Eliot is to rest considerable confidence on this question.) The feeling in the "Preludes" is a something separate from the awareness of them, a separation which a Whitman pursues backward through the multiplicity of Chinese-boxes, the "I's" of his poems. It is a *feeling* seeking a rest between *consciousness* and the *something* contained by consciousness. We as readers know that entity— that consciousness—through the images floating in it, the "forms" Wordsworth celebrates; and to the extent that we do, we break the walls of our own closed world, moved by pathos. By the act of the poem itself, Eliot keeps that possibility open, even as he concentrates upon the likelihood of illusion. In doing so, he pinpoints the central intellectual problem of his poetry, with an intensity which indicates it a very pressing, personal one which requires our consideration at some length.

NOTE

[1]Eliot, late in life, recalls his first encounter with Dante at the time of the "Preludes":

> There was one poet. . .who impressed me profoundly
> when I was twenty-two. . .one poet who remains the
> comfort and amazement of my age. . . In my youth, I
> think that Dante's astonishing economy and directness
> of language—his arrow that goes unerringly to the centre
> of the target—provided for me a wholsome corrective to
> the extravagances of the Elizabethan, Jacobean and
> Caroline authors in whom I also delighted.
>
> "To Criticize the Critic" (1961)

VI

THE SHIFTING SANDS OF EGO AND THE ROCK

You are not the same people who left that station
Or who will arrive at any terminus. . .

Dry Salvages

When we look closely at the emerging, eminent philosopher or scientist, he always appears to be the father of a new age. For we look closely at him in regard to his immediate effects. An Einstein, the philosopher of the modern world (despite his protests, those who approach him ask metaphysical questions), seems to have called into existence the world we find about us in the 1970s. But when we put such minds in a larger context, the philosopher seems rather a final flowering of a period: Plato of Athens; Augustine of Rome; Galileo of the medieval world; Einstein of the Renaissance. When our focus is sufficiently refined, we may see that the long-range effects such a mind enjoys reside not in the history of that cause-effect they influence but in that they raise abiding, timeless questions. It is in this respect that one of Eliot's early friends, Wyndham Lewis, attacks a too-limited examination of relativity by A. N. Whitehead and his followers, attempting to extricate the timeless questions from the historical matrix. A masterful ironist, Lewis establishes his credentials as exactly those of contemporary (1927) science. One need not be a mathematician, he says, to examine effects and question them, effect being the primary concern of current science. God, who was once the Cause of Causes, is now the Effect of Effects. But what Lewis notes is that in this shift of emphasis from cause to effect, science and philosophy alike are turning back to history and concentrating upon *power*. In the year of Lewis's own book, Bertrand Russell publishes a poor man's relativity in which the *power* of relativity is the new God. What the move means, therefore, is the secularization of the several muses, since the "effects" of science and philosophy permeate the arts. Lewis looks with a particularly scathing eye upon A. N. Whitehead's *Science and the Modern World* (1925), largely because of a dangerous innocence he detects in Whitehead, well-intentioned though he be.

In that book, one finds such passages as the following, perhaps a bit more to the point of our concern than the passages Lewis himself chooses. Whitehead says

> You are in a certain place perceiving things. Your
> perception takes place where you are, and is entirely
> dependent on how your body is functioning. But this
> functioning of the body in one place, exhibits for your
> cognisance an aspect of the distant environment, fading
> away into the general knowledge that there are things
> beyond. If this cognisance conveys knowledge of a
> transcendent world, it must be because the event which
> is the bodily life unifies in itself aspects of the universe.

He then goes on to establish a relation of his argument to the
perceptions of the poet of the nineteenth century.

> This is a doctrine extremely consonant with the vivid
> expression of personal experience which we find in the
> nature-poetry of imaginative writers such as Wordsworth
> and Shelley. The brooding, immediate presences of
> things are an obsession to Wordsworth. What the theory
> does do is to edge cognitive mentality away from being
> the necessary substratum of the unity of experience.
> That unity is now placed in the unity of an event. Ac-
> companying this unity, there may or may not be cogni-
> tion.

In other words, this constitutes an argument, supported by the
authority of the poet's intuition, for the separate existence of
the "cognitive mentality" and "the unity of an event." The
moment is thus given a real existence separate from cognition,
which is another way of affirming an objective reality to flux,
though Whitehead cannot finally establish the separation logically. Indeed, Lewis contends the difficulty to be that Whitehead is
making, not a scientific or philosophical argument, but an artistic
one. An artistic picture of the universe, furthermore, out of an
abstraction. Little wonder that Shelley is a poet he turns to in
pursuit of a moment of nature. In defense of flux as a means of
escaping the purely subjective impression of nature, establishment of a possible unity separate from cognition, he concentrates
(Lewis charges) on the accidents of perception, the so-called
secondary qualities of color, scent, sound, which suggest movement and change. But, Lewis asks, as *realists,* empiricists, what is
our strongest impression of the "out there," the world exterior
to perception? Not change, but stability. Without accounting
for this realization of immobility in nature, "the fastness and

deadness of nature," Whitehead's school have given us only a partial account of our experience of the external world. "Surely it is the abstraction of the materialistic picture of science that puts the movement and the fusion into [nature]?" Time as the mind of space stirs up the universe. It is, in effect, eighteenth century deism in scientific clothing. We are still trapped, the pathetic concomitants of that entrapment being displayed in the technique of *Ulysses* or *A la recherche du temps perdu.* And, we add to Lewis, displayed as well in the early poetry of Eliot, up to the drowned Phoenician in whose death the abiding question of the One and the Many is once more raised, but in terms of that intersection of history two thousand years ago which transformed both nature and Plato's old question of the One and the Many. We may look a bit further into the effects leading Eliot to his overwhelming question, borrowing Lewis's justification for such an examination of modern philosophy's and science's secularizing the muses of the intellect, feeling justified on their own ground no less than on the scriptural equivalent, "By their fruits ye shall know them." Whitehead's mystical pragmatism as a solution to our problem makes of the self a unified event in space or time. It allows for the rescue of a concept of organic progress, an infinite flow through entities—a mind for instance—in which the flow is at once subject and object, depending upon the perspective one has upon the entity at the moment. Entity is, then, a medium in which flux may be rationalized as flow, and some sense of direction and force rescued from the fears of chaos. But his "organic mechanism," which sees every part of the universe as a microcosm of correspondences to the whole, effectively destroys distinction, once the distinctiveness of his terms is assimilated and related to each other. That is what leads Eliot's friend Wyndham Lewis to a rather devastating analysis of Whitehead in "Romantic Art Called in to Assist in the Destruction of 'Materialism'," (*Time and Western Man*, 1927). Thus, avoiding the scholastic concept of the potential, which requires a cause separate from the closed universe, Whitehead writes, "The many feelings which belong to an incomplete phase in the process of an actual entity, though unintegrated by reason of the incompleteness of the phase, are compatible for synthesis by reason of the unity of their subject. . . The feeling is an episode in self-production, and is referent to its aim." This passage is from his *Process and Reality*, two years after Lewis' attack upon his "romanticism," and Whitehead is still in pursuit of a self-justified universe.

For one to arrive at the unity of an uncaused, self-supporting universe, potential must be replaced by *process.* Under
"Process" Whitehead remarks that "the flux of things is one
ultimate generalization around which we must weave our philosophical system." Flux is the absolute, the first cause out of which
entity (consciousness) must be at once derived and justified, and
the Incarnation of Flux seems to reside in the continuously
flickering effect, which fascinates and hypnotizes consciousness
as if a swinging light or mirror. The Manichaean dimension to
flux is supplied in its opposite, the "notion" of the "perma-
nences of things," as Whitehead puts it, as if answering Lewis's
earlier criticism. Metaphysics is the attempt to reconcile the
two. He cites as a union of the Heraclitian concept and the appe-
tite for permanence, between which individual awareness is torn,
not a philosophy but a hymn: "Abide with me/Fast falls the
eventide." He adds, "Here at length we find formulated the
complete problem of metaphysics." But the formulation itself
dissolves; for the image we depend upon partakes of both the
permanent and the transient. Naming arrests, but names decay
or distort: the flux of eventide, of the river; the permanence of
stone or mountain. Even the naming of *flux* denies the thing it
names, turning attention backward upon the namer, through an
examination of the images themselves. The flux of awareness
holds to the image, as if a permanent; yet we discover there is
flux in image, as it appears on the one hand a dead sign and on
the other living symbol. Neither *flux of things* or the *constant*
of an awareness of flux answers the problem. It is as if Whitehead were justifying the "Preludes" by answering Bradley's incompleteness. (He says in his "Preface" that he is in sharp disagreement with Bradley throughout.) In doing so he asserts a
solution to the problem of "feelings" that troubled Eliot so
heavily at the literary level in his early poems and essays. In
those early essays, the confusions in Eliot's term *feeling* become
particularly troublesome, since he is not willing to accept art as
purely subjective, as the state of philosophy and physics at that
moment seem to require. And yet he is not able to affirm objective existence either. Thus, while arguing the necessity of an
objective control of art if art is to escape the personal, he speaks
also of "various feelings, inhering for the writer in particular
words or phrases or images," whereby those feelings and words
together presumably enjoy an authority independent of the
"personality" of the poet. The phrase "for the writer" throws
the whole problem back into the subjective, since words cannot

be declared to bear those feelings (Whitehead has said "notions") independently in themselves. At another point of Eliot's argument *feeling* is a part of the furniture of the mind, the poet's mind being "a receptacle for seizing and storing up numberless feelings, phrases, images until all the particles which can unite to form a new compound are present together." When we consider that Eliot is writing not simply as poet but as a trained philosopher, we cannot accept as a resolution of this confusion the out that he is speaking as poet, that is, metaphorically. The question is whether *feeling* is an *image* of some universal truth inhering in the external world (which may or may not include the words), and is consequently superior to *emotion,* the term he counters to *feeling.* Is *emotion* the *feeling* (image) clouded by the personal? And it is a question Eliot is not yet prepared to answer.

At about the time Wyndham Lewis is criticizing Whitehead's *Science and the Modern World.* Eliot writes Bonamy Dobree words which show how far he has changed from the position reflected in the "Preludes":

> I would not wish to make truth a function of the will.
> On the contrary. I mean that if there is no fixed truth,
> there is no fixed object for the will to tend to. If truth
> is always changing, then there is nothing to do but to sit
> down and watch the pictures. . .and there can be no
> permanent reality if there is no permanent truth. . . For
> you cannot even say it changes except in reference to
> something which does not change; the idea of change is
> impossible without the idea of permanence.

Eliot will not rest in flux, which does not mean that the permanent is easy. Years later he will recall that old struggle as one which continues with one. It is not so easily resolved as it seemed in "Tradition and the Individual Talent," but neither is it cause for despair, even though it is without final solution this side the grave. He says, in *East Coker:*

> And so each venture
> Is a new beginning, a raid on the inarticulate
> With shabby equipment always deteriorating
> In the general mess of imprecision of feeling,
> Undisciplined squads of emotion.

What Whitehead does is pursue a mystical immanence, which Eliot has abandoned for transcendence to answer his problem, though he submits that mystical inclination to the rigors of reason and at great length. In his "Theory of Feeling" we find correspondences to the problem Eliot has examined in Bradley (in his dissertation) and in poets like Wordsworth (in "Tradition and the Individual Talent") and in himself (in his concern for the "objective correlative" and the "dissociation of sensibility"): the problem of distinguishing subject and object. Whitehead writes, "The 'effects' of an actual entity are its interventions in concrescent processes other than its own. Any entity, thus intervening in processes transcending itself, is said to function as an 'object'. . . A feeling cannot be abstracted from the actual entity entertaining it. The feelings are inseparable from the end at which they aim; and this end is the feeler. The feelings aim at the feeler, as their final cause. . . It is better to say that the feelings *aim at* their subject, than to say that they are *aimed at* their subject. For the latter mode of expression removes the subject from the scope of the feeling and assigns it to an external agency. Thus the feeling would be abstracted from its own final cause. The actual entities share with God this characteristic of self-causation. For this reason every actual entity also shares with God the characteristic of transcending all other actual entities, including God. The universe is thus a creative advance into novelty."

But if one look at the "entity" which is the consciousness of Eliot's "Preludes," he sees that the problem engaged is exactly whether the consciousness is the final cause which the feelings *aim at* or whether the entity isn't rather a first cause, and the feeling a sort of whistling in the dark. That entity is "moved by fancies that are curled" about images, and there are "feelings" of some infinitely suffering and patient thing; but the relation of *feeling* to *entity* and *thing* is unresolved. Whitehead's suggested resolution seems open to the same objection Pascal raises to Descartes's use of the term God: "in his whole philosophy he would like to do without God; but he could not help allowing him a flick of the fingers to set the world in motion." (We might remember also Pascal's scorn of Cartesianism, before the emergence of romanticism in literature: Descartes's is "the Romance of Nature" which is "something like the story of Don Quixote.") What Whitehead doesn't seem to have provided is some way of seeing and accepting an actual entity's participation in concrescent processes other than its own, so that the seeing and accepting may be divorced from the entity and process, the seeing in this instance being Whitehead's. This objection is analogous to C. S. Lewis's in his criticism of Freudianism when he says it can account for everything but Freud. Still, Whitehead is in pursuit of a still point no less than Eliot, and in the direction Eliot initially embarks upon. But the difficulty which Eliot requires an accounting of is to explain how one steps out of the stream of process, out of "entity," to stand upon the banks of being and assert being. What is that existence standing or sitting by the tumid river; it is clearly a particularity. (Whitehead is just such a particularity through whom issues *Process and Reality*.) The consequences of the present moment in London as a continuum of the past moment stretch forward as well; Narcissus cannot quite ignore either past or future. "Memory!" Eliot exclaims in "Rhapsody of a Windy Night," "You have the key,/The little lamp spreads a ring on the stair."

And *Cogito ergo sum* is a trick. As Brice Parain says, in *A Metaphysics of Language,* "Why not. . .invert the *cogito* and say: I think, therefore I am not. For to think is not to be, it is to wish to be. . . To think is to struggle painfully in lies and errors, to struggle against them, to escape from them." When one's thought is in the stream of immanence, when the overwhelming question of the One and the Many is reduced from the transcendent to the Self and the Other, to a *closed* system, reality can be only process in *a* conscious entity and nothing more. The hollowness of that victory lies in its only possible absolute—absolute alienation. It is our inheritance of that strange amalgamation of eighteenth century rationalism which mixes Platonic Idealism with empiricism, a more disturbed philosophical period than we are yet accustomed to acknowledge it, primarily because it is so largely credited as the father of Progress, whom we worship as one of the greater gods.

Whitehead's New-Pythagorean music, which labors to reconcile physics to philosophy, is a persuasive music so long as the music goes on. When the music stops, when the discourse is ended, the old problem yet remains. We become aware of ourselves by the waters of Leman, exiled out of the wholeness we thought to justify. Again, as Parain puts the dilemma which so engages the modern world: "All difficulties of philosophy arise from the fact that we constantly have two pictures of ourselves, what we feel and what we say, and from our not immediately knowing why there must be two and not one." The struggle is to justify the "I" that contains both pictures. Eliot reaches the point where he cannot credit either philosophy or science with solution to that burning question, turning then to St. Augustine to understand that exile which he will accept in "Ash-Wednesday," as he begins to climb the stair with the light of memory and hunger of desire. Indeed Augustine, before Descartes, has wrestled with our question of personal identity as with most of our problems. He asserts with a confidence of conclusion that

> . . .without any delusive representation of images or phantasms, I am most certain that I am, that I know, and that I delight in this. On none of these points do I fear the arguments of the skeptics of the Academy who say: what if you are deceived? For if I am deceived, I am. For he who does not exist cannot be deceived; and if I am deceived, by this same token I am. And since I am if I am deceived, how am I deceived in believing that I am?. . . Consequently, neither am I deceived in knowing that I know. For, as I know that I am, so I know also, that I know.

Augustine pursues his point to establish the existence of awareness, so that he may turn the concern of awareness back to that which is separate from it, and from which it is separated by its own failure. He directs the quest to a light larger than that upon the broken columns of the civilization around him, the unreal city of his own day which echoes so disturbingly in our own world.

In the uneasy pursuit of the "relevant" for our moment, his justification of the self and redirecting it to the light is surely a place to start. One may reflect upon the ironic appropriation and manipulation by our young of the terms which immanence settles into finally—a pragmatic world given to an assertion of the self's powers, with the self as its own end. The cry that one is *"doing* his own *thing"* is a metaphor for the pursuit of "being oneself," an assertion of existence, and it carries the desperate cry for an end to which to direct being, an end which is higher than the self, so that one is not reduced to the conclusion that "there is nothing to do but sit down and watch the pictures."

The modern quest for a rest of the self in something larger than itself can be perverted, but it does not mean we are so unlike other ages as we sometimes seem to hope. The spectacular perversions of being by the Manson "family" are more sensational than unique to human history. But having justified the self, one may rely on memory as some guide out of *The Waste Land,* rely on history. We observe thereby that, in any period where the self is disoriented from its attempt to find rest in some transcendent, aberrations occur.   The children's crusades of the 1960s or of the thirteenth century are symptoms of a malady abroad and infecting individual spirits.   A Montferrat, a Gilles de Rais, a Charles Manson are instances of but one of the directions spiritual discomfort may take. White magic is the benign aspect of black, capable it is true of turning malignant; and the flourishing of astrology, of occultism such as embraces both the malign and benign selves among us, is cause at once of despair and hope, those inescapable twin conditions of the self in the world. That is why it is worth looking somewhat further into an instance of the malignant, a far less spectacular specimen than Gills de Rais or Charles Manson, but in respect to the malady of the individual soul no less dangerous and most appropriate to our concern with *The Waste Land* since the subject was a friend of Eliot's. It will seem rather sensational on my part to associate Eliot's "Mr. Apollinax"—son of Apollo—with these vicious destroyers of the body such as Manson, but if one consider the fate of the soul as far more important than that of the body, as Augustine and Dante did and as Eliot came to do, the alarm may be justified precisely because the danger is less obvious, more subtle. To make this approach will also allow us some reflection upon a naiveté in Eliot at the beginning, a condition he may be said to have outgrown in the writing of *The Waste Land.* In that growth we may see why Eliot could not maintain himself in the same intellectual country as our present subject, Bertrand Russell, can be said to have plundered.

As Russell's *Autobiography* (and evidence in other of his writings) demonstrates, he has the inclination, but lacks the wit, to be our age's Voltaire. Consequently he settles for a Byronic pose, through which he perpetuates a pagan innocence. His pragmatic solution to the mind's problem—that is, to declare those problems uninteresting—accounts for his split with A. N. Whitehead, with whom he collaborated on what is (in refined opinion) his major work, *Principia Mathematica.* Of the body of his work other than mathematical—his writings on manners, morals, marriage, education, politics—one might consider Wyndham Lewis's summary judgment, in *Time and Western Man:* "My main accusation against Mr. Russell is. . .that his mind is that of an excited and rather sentimental amateur, bursting for mild 'sensations,' for things that are 'amusing' and that will surprise his intelligence into activity. . . He is a sort of born entertainer: and his entertainer's instinct has always led him to take the entertaining or 'exciting' side in the debate. . .'amusement' is. . .the word that must come most often into any analysis of the springs of such an intelligence as that of Mr. Russell." The date of these remarks is 1927, some forty years before the Stockholm circus of the War Crimes Tribunal. But long before Lewis's remarks, Eliot reflects vague intimations of the showman in Russell, in "Mr. Apollinax." In the poem, Eliot is more taken with the shock to New England sensibility of the obvious Dionysiac element in this Son of Apollo—with the Boston ladies' reaction to his "pointed ears" and the hovering threat of Priapus, than with reconciling that disparity himself. There is the delightful play of these ladies making riot with Mr. Apollinax like Bacchantes, tearing him apart with their proper, refined words. Still a D. H. Lawrence, hardly one in whom resides the same sensibility, will see the same disparity (in 1915-16) and say of him to Lady Asquity: "Bertie Russell talks about democratic control and the education of the artisan and all this. . .goodness is just a warm and cosy cloak for a bad spirit. . . What does Russell really want? He wants to keep his own established ego, his finite and ready-defined self intact, free from contact and connection." Herbert Howarth says of Russell that he has the gift of restating "the most difficult systems. . .plainly in a familiar vocabulary." As a translator of philosophy, we may compare him to Pound, the translator of poetry, and see justification of Lawrence's suspicions of Russell. For, as he reveals in talking of his books in the *Autobiography,* he is interested largely in the power money will give him. His contempt of Americans is heightened when they don't buy his current book in sufficient numbers to keep him in his accustomed manner. Though incisively critical of Russell's position, Conrad treats Russell more kindly on his egotistical solutions to world social and political problems than that wild direct spirit D. H. Lawrence will consent to do. (See Conrad's letter in the second volume of Russell's *Autobiography.*) But Lawrence writes Russell (September 1915): "You are really the super-war-spirit," and quotes to him a woman who heard a lecture against war, " 'It seemed so strange, with his face looking so evil, to be talking about peace and love.' " And indeed there is a disparity which Eliot's and Lawrence's ladies seem to have sensed. Russell in his *Autobiography* recalls writing a book to refute both Marx and classical economists (*Power: A New Social Analysis*) and in the next paragraph congratulates himself on pitting two potential buyers of some property against each other. "In twenty-four hours, owing to their competition, I succeeded in increasing the price they offered by 1000." He recalls solving a problem of conscience over some debentures he owned in an English engineering company engaged in England's behalf during World War I: he gave them to Eliot, at the same time excoriating Eliot for being in sympathy with the English. After the war, Eliot gave them back. "Oh keep the dog far hence," and let us have none but honest wolves. But since that cannot be, let us look a bit further into the concept of power to which Russell is attracted and consider its prospects for humanity. Another of Russell's contemporaries spent much of his energy and art doing precisely that. During the 1920s Aldous Huxley looked with devastating eye upon the world of London intellectual society of which Eliot was inhabitant. It is the period of his own involvement with that world upon which Eliot will cast the lamp of memory and in 1934 confide to Dobree of his role in it, "I don't think my poetry is any good: . . .nothing but a brilliant future behind me." Less playfully he will recall that period and the subsequent decade, in *East Coker*, as

> Twenty years largely wasted, the years *l'entre deux
>   guerres—*
> Trying to learn to use words.

VII

USUAL PASTIMES:
LORD RUSSELL AND MADAM SOSOSTRIS

                    All these are usual
Pastimes and drugs, and features of the press:
And always will be, some of them especially
When there is distress of nations and perplexity
Whether on the shores of Asia, or in Edgware Road.

Dry Salvages

The iconoclast has a decided advantage over mortals. In dealing with the silliness of mankind, he is free to play the bright light of his wit in a generous and general melting glow upon the holy and unholy alike and yet not fade into the somberness of that dark cloud of concern in a Swift. On the other hand he must not allow light to burn too hot with the searing evangelical puritanism of a Mencken or Ezra Pound. With some gift, the iconoclast suspends folly in amber so that it endures not so much because one accepts it as high truth highlighted but as weakness preserved, against which we measure ourselves with the perpetual entertainment of that unchidden Pharisee whom on occasion we all discover in ourselves. The best iconoclast's work appears dated to us in the degree to which we wish not to be implicated in folly, but he has a disturbing habit of being with us always. In the 1970s he is Tom Wolfe, a brilliant smart aleck, with an acute sense of the absurd. Apparently without Swift's curse of a commitment to the human race and without Chaucer's humorous sympathy for human foibles, he makes our world his meat. Any facet of our life may find itself juxtaposed to itself or to some other in a ridiculous and telling joining. Cesar Chavez or Leonard Bernstein, whose side is he on? A question not to be asked, for once answered the iconoclast is out of business.

In 1921, *Radical Chic & Mau-Mauing the Flak Catchers* was called *Crome Yellow,* and it was written by Aldous Huxley. Himself a frequenter of Lady Ottoline Morrell's country home at Garsington, he was in an admirable position to observe and record the Leonard Bernstein circle of his day. For D. H. Lawrence, Virginia Woolf, T. S. Eliot, Bertrand Russell are but a sampling of her compendious salon, which others have also given us pictures of. Eliot captures something of that world in "The Game of Chess," and it is a major concern in Pound's angry excoriation of London as Unreal City, *Hugh Selwyn Mauberley: Life and Contacts.* Eliot tried to capture it closer to Huxley's own mode in those eighteenth century couplets he discarded from the final version of *The Waste Land,* but so various and disjoint is that world that one can hardly imagine verse up to the task.   Huxley's prose provides the better medium, and an entrance more revealing of that world at the hortatory level of our concern.   Consequently, his novel is more helpful to our seeing Eliot's uneasiness with a local world which drifts (to our puzzlement) through *The Waste Land.*   In short, the narrative mode, with its implications of orderly revelation and development, makes the better foil to comic absurdity than does the mythical mode.

The setting is Crome, the country home of Henry and Priscilla Wimbush, through which flows the intellectual and spiritual society of the day.   Crome itself dates from the days of Elizabeth.   Its builder (as Henry discovers in his researches for a *History of Crome,* published on his own press) was preoccupied with one thought, "The proper placing of his privies," an obsession that accounts for the three towers of the building, in which those conveniences were housed.   Henry, who likes people in books and not in person, occupies himself with setting down minute details of those generations from Sir Ferdinando Lapith down to his own grandfather.   He is, one might say with Huxley's weakness for the outrageous, fascinated by this house so deeply steeped in history.   And in one passage Huxley allows himself a lush richness in describing the bed and room in which the Wimbush's niece Anne lies, a passage in its effect strikingly like that of the opening lines of "The Game of Chess" in its presentation of withered stumps of time.   It is a "nice" counterpointing to the less seemly side of Crome's history.

The Wimbushes and Mr. Scogan form a triangle of the older generation, a ménage à trois, around whom flows a variety of young spirits, the most important one being the young poet Denis Stone.   Mr. Wimbush has his mind anchored in the dead past.   The spectacular trophy of his researches he shows Denis late at night, while traditional country dance is under way on the manor grounds: logs hollowed out as conduits for Sir Fernando's privies.   Priscilla Wimbush on the other hand drifts in the flux of the present moment; "for consolation she dallied with New Thought and the Occult."   Mr. Scogan puts the two together, past and present, and envisages a future in which rational man will come at last into his own.   The devastating fun begins.

On one long, dull evening of her perpetual house-party,

Priscilla Wimbush remarks to one of her guests, Mr. Barbecue-Smith, author of *Pipe-Lines to the Infinite,* "This Einstein theory. It seems to upset the whole starry universe. It makes me so worried about my horoscope." It is rather clear from the texture Huxley weaves for us that her universe is one out of Eliot's early poetry. We are in a vacant lot at Crome; several worlds of suspended ego revolve, hardly aware of each other except as objects to reflect themselves. How dare Einstein disturb such universes which drift oblivious of all else. However, Mr. Scogan, whom Huxley carefully divests of family and title (a point of small importance we shall come to), can see the marvelous possibilities of that new world dawning. He seizes upon Denis, not because of his imagination but his innocence, as a sounding board and possible convert. Tomorrow rational mind will come into its own, manipulating society to its own ends, he promises. Mr. Scogan is divorced of nature and humanity, as he says of himself, preferring to travel in the subway whenever possible, the man made thing. He can look at society as raw material to which he may apply his logical formulae, and he sketches possibilities which Huxley is to adumbrate with more terror in *Brave New World.* Huxley, like Denis Stone, was to lose that innocence which in 1921 still allowed him to draw his devastating caricatures.

Though Huxley is writing a novel, the principals of Lady Ottoline Morrell's circle at Garsington, post World War I society, are more or less recognizable even at this remove. As Eliot remarks of the book in his memorial note on Huxley in 1965, they appear there "under the thinnest of disguises." The Morrell-Wimbushes share a commune, a Canada for the day to which pacifists migrate to work the land idealistically. Mr. Scogan describes the project as "practical" and "eminently realistic." "In this farm we have a model of sound paternal government. Make them breed, make them work, and when they're past working or breeding or begetting, slaughter them." There is a vague uneasiness about the matter, which results from the ambiguity of whether Mr. Scogan is speaking of pigs and cattle or of the people of whom Huxley was one in the historical experiment he appropriates to his fiction.

The most interesting of our characters is Mr. Scogan, whose disguise, when we can penetrate it, provides us much to say in relation to Mrs. Wimbush's "next world and all the spirits" that are her highest concern at the moment. We have said that Huxley is careful to have Mr. Scogan disclaim family history and possibilities of title, which strategy one may imagine for the sake of our argument a matter of disguise. He is, among those gathered at Crome, eminently logical. He spins arguments on sex, on animal husbandry (for both human and farm animals), on man's place in the universe. He lectures at some length on man's determinist entrapment, arguing that "no holiday is ever anything but a disappointment" because of that entrapment. He is a most disturbing element in Denis's encounter with the outer world, since Denis is in pursuit of love, he thinks, in the person of Anne. Mr. Scogan coldly and persuasively reduces the individual to an integer of force. If he is not one to lecture on Einstein's Special Theory of Relativity and its corallaries, he is in his thinking nevertheless hand in glove with its possibilities as a blueprint of practical force in society.

When Denis becomes emotionally distraught over Anne's relationship with a Lawrence-like painter, Mr. Scogan lectures him at length on the possibilities of rationality. And at a point when Anne and Denis are at last in a most intimate emotional relationship, Mr. Scogan comes and literally settles his world between them, forcing them to give him room to sit between them. His world is that of the "Rational State," just over the horizon, as he confides to Denis. In it there will be "Directing Intelligencies," who will have under them the "Men of Faith," to be used in whipping up enthusiasm in the "herd," for whatever project those Intelligencies have under way. The Men of Faith are maniacs, and since "everything that ever gets done in this world is done by madmen" (Luther and Napoleon in Mr. Scogan's list, to which we may add a Jerry Rubin or two), they are to be the intermediaries, instruments to the reconstruction of the world. Eccentricity, Mr. Scogan holds, is glorious, being the only justification of aristocracy, and he calculates his own eminence in that remnant of the self-elect. If the male guests each have assigned to them (by Mr. Scogan) one of the first six Caesars as prototype, Mr. Scogan is himself "potentially all of them. . .with the possible exception of Claudius, who was much too stupid to be a development of anything in my character." And as if to prove it in part, he confides to the lovelorn Denis that he can see no place in the Rational State for such as he. "No, I can see no place for you; only the lethal chamber."

Under the shock of this rejection of the poet of love from the rationalist's new *Republic,* Denis finds himself looking into the sketchbook of another guest, the shy, unnoticed Jenny, who from the beginning his pronounced Mr. Scogan "slightly sinister." In her private "Fable of the Wallflower and the Sour Grapes," Denis discovers a devastating picture of Crome. Her sketches show Mr. Scogan as more than "slightly sinister. . .indeed, diabolic." Denis's own self-centered world is fractured by the sketches of himself he sees there. Where before he could maintain that it is "impossible that other people should be in their way as elaborate and complete as he [in his world]," Jenny's red notebook has "put beyond a doubt the fact that the outer world really existed," for she has been able to see Denis in a light he recognizes as valid. Mr. Scogan, who can comfort Denis by the assurance that "there's no ultimate point to existence," can allow himself to assume the mask of fortune teller to the peasants on Bank Holiday, at the local charity fair, but Denis can only wander about this new world his eyes are opening to, becoming more desolate and confused as illusions are dissolved. In this new version of Vanity Fair, he finds himself attracted by curiosity to the terrifying "outer world," and particularly to the fortune teller's tent. There Mr. Scogan, dressed as a woman, is billed as "Sesostris, the Sorceress of Ecbatana." Denis, eavesdropping, hears him predict her seduction to a country girl, one of the lesser members of the Herd. It is a dark prediction of rape which so titillates the girl that she hungers for all the gory details. But "Madam Sesostris" will only say, looking intently at her plam, "I cannot predict what will happen after that."

Huxley was inevitably asked (by Grover Smith) whether there was any relation between his Madam Sesostris, and Eliot's Madam Sosostris. He couldn't say whether Eliot was familiar with *Crome Yellow* or not, but he himself borrowed the material from *Jane Eyre.* But the more interesting question is who hides under the disguise of Madam Sesostris more than Mr. Scogan. If Mr. Scogan, constantly shown puffing his pipe and submitting all remarks to witty scrutiny, isn't Bertrand Russell, he is close enough to serve the purpose. Nor can one help remarking how close Jenny's and Denis's reading of the seemingly gentle Mr. Scogan corresponds to D. H. Lawrence's reading of the seemingly gentle, peace-loving Russell in 1915.

If we look at Mr. Scogan's solace in the new world dawning, which so assures him that there is "no ultimate point of existence," one sees the position not as a belief but as an instrument for bringing a world into process. An Einstein may upset the starry universe and in the light of his own ideas choose to deny the apparent implications by reasserting a humility which holds that all is not yet known: "I cannot believe that God plays dice with the world." But with God safely removed, Mr. Scogan can take up that game of dice as one of the Directing Intelligences.   All is not known, but enough to assure power. Huxley sees this side of Russell more clearly and directly, at a point in time where the clouds are gathering over Europe. He writes E. M. Forster (February 17, 1935):

> Bertie Russell, whom I've just been lunching with, says one oughtn't to mind about the superficial things like ideas, manners, politics, even wars—that the really important things, conditioned by scientific technique, go steadily on and up. . .in a straight, un-undulating trajectory.   It's nice to think so; but. . .who knows if that straight trajectory isn't aiming directly for some fantastic denial of humanity?

That is, of course, the shocking insight young Denis Stone experiences at Crome, just after World War I. It awakens him to a realization of his Prufrockian state in which his soul is "a tenuous, tremulous, pale membrane." He says to the flighty Mary Bracegirdle, who understands not a word he says (any more than he understands the painful personal situation she is in), "The individual. . .is not a self-supporting universe. There are times when he comes into contact with other individuals, when he is forced to take cognisance of the existence of other universes besides himself. . ." The "Einstein theory" is indeed well on its way to upsetting Denis's own "starry universe," and one of its effects will be to make him admit the waste land he inhabits, and try to find a way out of it.

But the way out is not so easy as taking "a very good train at 3.27," as Mary Bracegirdle leads him to do. Eliot, another frequenter of Lady Ottoline's salon, has already discovered that truth. By 1921 the implications of the Special Theory of Relativity, first propounded as Eliot is about to set off for Harvard in 1905, and soon to be made popular by Bertrand Russell in his

The ABC of Relativity (two years before Eliot announces himself royalist, Tory, Catholic), have worked deeply into thought.
The latest eruption of that theory has caused intellectual and
spiritual panic to our world, in ways more pervasive than the
spectacle of the atomic bomb. But to burst the atom may be
no more startling than to burst the ego's world, at least to the
burst ego—as Denis Stone discovered through Jenny and Mr.
Scogan. It is a discovery Eliot makes through *The Waste Land*,
in which the self-love of self-awareness sustains a deadly blow.
The preliminaries to that discovery are already behind Eliot when
he meets Virginia Woolf and other literati at Lady Ottoline's
salon, where he is brought by Bertrand Russell.

We see Eliot, in his early poetry, exploring the problem of a
dramatic level of action beneath the level of time-space, and so
beneath the uses of the narrative method he was struggling to
discard. One of the escapes from that narrative method is into
the abstractions of philosophy, though that line of pursuit would
seem to take one more and more away from the world within the
world he is riddling, the "awareness" within or without the
"other." To state the problem in such terms is already to have
gained such a separation from the experience one is pursuing as
to make that experience necessarily vicarious. How does one
"act" out the problem and so solve it? Eliot is not the first,
nor will he be the last, to see poetry as a means of resolving
that mysterious question. He vacillates, then, between philosophy and poetry, and one is initially startled to see just how ex-
tensive is his bibliography of philosophical book reviews and
essays between the publication of "Prufrock" and *The Waste
Land.* In that period his publications on philosophical and, sub
genera, historical subjects outweigh his purely literary produc-
tion. He writes on Turgenev, Henry James, contemporary
poets, but he is also interested in Russell's *Mysticism and Logic,*
in Diderot as philosopher, in *Theism and Humanism, The Philosophy of Nietzsche,* William James, Leibniz, R. G. Colling-
wood. One scanning the topics of his book reviews and essays
of the period might suppose it probable on the evidence that he
would eventually give up vers libre for the life of a professor of
philosophy, as his mother hoped he might. But his concern is
more single than its showing forth in the literary, philosophical,
historical reviews might seem. It is the problem of escape from
the only absolute that either relativity or phenomenology seem
to leave open: absolute subjectivity. (Unlike Eliot, Bertrand

Russell may well chuckle over the comedy of philosophy and physics in a new Berkeleyan world. After all, that circumstance makes it at last probable, even practicable, that Plato's *Republic* can be brought about, since the anchor of that possible world is no longer in the transcendent but only in the mind of man— someone like Mr. Scogan for instance.)

If Einstein can overthrow the Newtonian absolute of un- moveable space, which had served as Primum Mobile of the scientist's world—and along with it overthrow absolute time— Leibniz has been there before him and in such a way as to make thought itself a part of the world foreshadowed by the Special Theory of Relativity. Given space as the order or relation of things among themselves and time as simply a possible order of events, what then is mind in relation to time-space? Eliot is con- cerned with exactly this problem in his "Development of Leib- niz' Monadism," published in the *Monist* in 1916. Summarizing Leibniz' concept, he concludes that by it one is given to under- stand that "matter is an arrested moment of mind, 'mind without memory.' By state is not meant feeling but the monad at an in- stant of time." Though the question Leibniz raises begins in physical force, "monad" is located in body, and "hence a ten- dency to psychologism, to maintain that ideas always find their home in particular minds, that they have a psychological as well as a logical existence. Leibniz on this side opened the way for modern idealism." One sees that Eliot means by "mod- ern idealism" an idealism from which the transcendent or its possibility is excluded, one which meets the new physics on its own grounds. And it is the direction in which one moves to justify an assumption of power in order to manipulate the order of objects and their suspense, including people as objects. It makes no difference to that assumption whether God plays dice with the universe or not; such a question, indeed, is beside the point to modern idealism. Except to an Einstein or Eliot.

If space is but the order or relation of things among them- selves, may one suppose that proposition to be also one way of describing consciousness? Put another way, is consciousness a relation of images (including perceptions—whatever those are) among themselves? And put yet another way, we have Eliot's "Preludes" and "Rhapsody on a Windy Night" and "The Love Song of J. Alfred Prufrock." The old materials of poetry's narrative action—metaphors of seasons or history's ages—no

longer suffice.   Not only must one abandon the "narrative
method," but also the illusions of pattern in those images held
in the mind.

> Whispering lunar incantations
> Dissolve the floors of memory
> And all its clear relations,
> Its divisions and precisions.

Memory itself is suspect since it is memory which encourages
the illusion of "clear relations."   It is not a fundamental "I"
in the awareness which is the ordering cause, but instead "Midnight" which

> shakes the memory
> As a madman shakes a dead geranium.

One can trust the memory only to "throw up high and dry/A
crowd of twisted things. . .twisted branch. . .broken spring in a
factory yard."   "Memory" is the "buried life" which will not
come back to life.   The situation to such a mind that wrestles
with this problem is desperate.   For, although such relativity
"works" in one's logic of the problem, it leaves one unsatisfied
as to the truth of the matter.   So too did Newton's fixed space
work; so too did the nineteenth century conception of light as a
fluid, a conception which contributed so heavily to the rise of
industrialism which leaves awareness crying desolately in city
streets.   It is not enough to have "had the experience but missed
the meaning."

  Neither Einstein nor Eliot will reject the ultimate questions
which rise from one's dissatisfaction with mathematics, philosophy, or poetry as The Way of getting at reality.   They object,
with Wallace Stevens's unimaginative men in the street, "You
have a blue guitar,/You do not play things as they are."   Stevens,
content with poetry as a border of ideas, can have that objection
answered very much as Bertrand Russell answers it.   "Things as
they are/Are changed upon the blue guitar."   But the presumption of validity in that answer in Stevens leads to music of an
exquisitely delightful kind while in Russell it must lead inevitably
to Huxley's *Brave New World*.   We see this in the concluding
chapter of his *ABC of Relativity*.   There Russell talks about the
new doctrine in its "Philosophical Consequences," and we find

ourselves back at Crome and Garsington in the final sentences:

> Assuming the utmost that can be claimed for physics, it
> does not tell us what it is that changes or what are its
> various states; it only tells us such things as that changes
> follow each other periodically, or spread with a certain
> speed. . . To the non-mathematical mind, the abstract
> character of our physical knowledge may seem unsatis-
> factory. From an artistic or imaginative point of view,
> it is perhaps regrettable, but from a practical point of
> view it is of no consequence. Abstraction, difficult as
> it is, is the source of power. . .[A fianancier] . . .can deal
> in wheat or cotton without needing ever to have seen
> either; all he needs to know is whether they will go up
> or down.

Russell concludes with enthusiasm, where fear and trembling
were in better order, "it is astonishing that so little knowledge
can give us so much power."

Mr. Scogan couldn't put it better, and Huxley was surely
expressing an incisive portrait of Russell when he calls him, in
a letter to brother Julian in April of 1918, "a twentieth century
Godwin." A man who can conclude that "when we have been
told how things are electrified, and under what circumstances
they are electrified, we have been told all there is to tell" is
no man to trust in matters of light, most particularly the light of
the mind. Fortunately, though Eliot was a protegé of Russell's,
for whom Russell takes sometimes less, sometimes more credit,
he was not content with a pragmatic interest in power, in what is
going up or down, whether wheat, cotton, or political ideas. But
had Eliot remained as naive as he was initially, when Russell
undertook the psycho-physiological rewiring of his marriage to
Vivien, Eliot might have ended up at Russell's personal version of
Vanity Fair, as a chief justice of the war crime trials staged in
Stockholm. Since he did not, we still have much more to say of
his pursuit of light, a pursuit in the direction Mrs. Wimbush
wishes to move, out of the pathetic arrested moment of the
present. She can be captivated by Barbecue-Smith and his
fascinating comparison of "the Soul to a Lotus Pool." Denis,
the poet in love, the poet as Saint Narcissus endlessly crucified,
can see at last that Mr. Barbecue-Smith as writer of *Pipe-Lines to
the Infinite* and Mr. Scogan with his blueprint for the Rationalist

State are rather more closely akin than they at first seem to be. *The Power of Positive Thinking* and *The ABC of Relativity* are both interested in power. Einstein's theory may so upset the whole starry universe that it makes Priscilla worry over her horoscope; but, inundated by the crest of the present, she is a welcomed conductor of power into the social order, by a Mr. Scogan, ungrounded though she be. (As she says, "And then there's the next world and all the spirits, and one's Aura, and Mrs. Eddy and saying you're not ill, and the Christian Mysteries and Mrs. Besant. It's all splendid. One's never dull for a moment.") The more difficult way, Eliot's, is sometimes dull, but not uninteresting. Nor does he make that journey at random but requires a recapitulation constantly, a revisiting of memory to its garden where dead geraniums may not be dead after all. That is why he revisits Leibniz to discover where something went wrong in modern thought.

Leibniz asserts that he is "able to prove that not only light, color, heat, and the like, but motion, shape, and extension too are mere apparent qualities." And in his wake, Berkeley could assure us in a new psalm to the Creator that "all the choir of heaven and furniture of earth, in a word all those bodies which compose the mighty frame of the world, have not any substance without the mind. . . So long as they are not actually perceived by me, or do not exist in my mind, or that of any other created spirit, they must either have no existence at all, or else subsist in the mind of some Eternal Spirit." Then two subsequent arguments effectively removed Berkeley's Eternal Spirit from scientific and philosophical thought in the nineteenth and early twentieth century: Darwinian evolutionary theory, with its determinist aura, and Einstein's theory of relativity, which extended Berkeley by positing time and space as subjective perception. From a climate of mind which clung to the assurance that no sparrow falls but that God knows it, we wake into a world which concludes that, if the finite mind does not perceive the sparrow, it does not even exist. We accomplish, it seems, a resolution of that ancient enigma Plato phrases for us in the *Parmenides*, the riddle of the One and the Many, through a conception of the finite mind as the One in which the Many are resolved. That is, we secularize Plato. But such *unity* means the loss of *identity*. To assert a unity of existence in the individual mind leads to the destruction of the "I" each mind strives to protect and be comfortable with. Whitman's recessive pursuit of the "I" in his poetry is the corollary to the Leibniz-Berkeley-Einstein pursuit of unity into the dark continent of the interior where Freud and Jung were to establish trading posts. *I perceive an object. But what is it that perceives the "I's" relation to that object? Another "I"?* And so the crayfishing against the current of consciousness in "Song of Myself," the seeking of stable identity, to solve the terror of alienation in consciousness. To substitute *morning,* or *evening,* or *street* for the "I", as Eliot does in his "Preludes" is but a kind of shorthand and not a solution. Interestingly enough, an aid to the solution of the poet's dilemma of the "I" has come in part from an unexpected quarter, physics itself, which had seemed its enemy in Russell's reading of the relationship. For it has had to deal with a metaphysical question (without always realizing it a metaphysical one): what is the cause of the order of our perceptions and conceptions, so curiously consistent, if existence depends entirely upon the perceiving-conceiving, finite awareness? Physics has found itself required to make an assertion, an acceptance on faith, of existence as independent of finite perception-conception. Once one makes that physicist's version of Pascal's wager, Pascal's wager on God's existence is not far behind. Eternal Being re-enters the equation of $E = mc^2$, and the Voice of that Calling in *Little Gidding* is being heard louder and louder in the cloud chambers of the particle physicist. We find ourselves on the borders of a new Age of Faith, to which Eliot served as poet-prophet.

* * * * *

Since these pages were composed I have come upon corroborative evidence of Russell as prototype of Scogan, in Peter Fairchow's *Aldous Huxley: Satirist and Novelist* (University of Minnesota Press, 1972). Fairchow notes (p. 58) that "according to the annotations made by T. S. Eliot in his copy of *Crome Yellow,* Denis is Huxley himself and Scogan is 'Russell' (presumably Bertrand), though in his Paris Review interview Huxley explicitly stated that Scogan's character was based on Norman Douglas." Russell, according to Ronald Clark, took himself to be the original from whom Huxley drew his character and objected on the grounds that he was made "to put forward seriously the very ideas which he, Russell, had discussed as a joke at one of Lady Ottoline's house-parties" (*The Huxleys,* 1968). It is curious that in his *Autobiography* Russell mentions Huxley only once in all its pages since he knew Huxley through the years in a most personal way. That instance is the quotation of a one-sentence note from Huxley expressing sympathy when there was a public outcry over Russell's being given a position at the College of the City of New York. The grounds of the outcry Russell considers to equate him with Socrates: i.e., that he is falsely accused as potentially a corrupter of youth, but Huxley's own objections to Russell are on less shallow grounds than those of the suit against the College of the City of New York for his removal. In January of 1930, about the time he was writing *Brave New World,* Huxley wrote Scudder Klyce:

> The habit of the scientists was and still is to assert that the theories which work in the particular category of phenomena which they have chosen, arbitrarily, to consider, must work in all categories and conversely that the phenomenal categories in which these theories don't, as a matter of observed fact, work are for that reason illusory, non-existent. Hence the science-religion dispute, hence all the stoical despair of such professional despairers as Bertrand Russell. I can only find it all rather comic—though also tiresome.

It would appear that "Denis" still sees problems in "Scogan's" position. He has moved in a direction not widely divergent from Eliot's, though they are still considerably apart. He adds in the same letter:

> Being an unmetaphysically-minded person preoccupied with phenomenal appearances, not ultimate reality, I think mostly of the diverse Many and not much of the final One." (*Letters,* p. 325)

By the mid-1930s Huxley was turning more sharply away toward Eastern thought than seemed acceptable to Eliot. He writes Eliot, in response to Eliot's criticism of his position (July 1936):

> I quite agree with you that meditation requires a metaphysical or theological background. . . There is a very well informed and interesting book by a Catholic priest, Fr Bede Frost. . .which summarizes the very numerous

techniques of meditation evolved at different times during
the last five centuries. There are also a number of distinct
techniques among the Indians, Chinese and Tibetans.

It is clear enough from this letter that, while he can agree with
Eliot on the necessity of a metaphysic, he will not accept media-
tion. That is, he cannot be Christian. He writes in the same
month to Mrs. Kethevan Roberts, on the techniques of mental
prayer, that its effect

> will be modified to some extent by the nature of the
> underlying metaphysics, which may regard the substratum
> of the universe as personal or impersonal. It seems to me
> (a) truer and (b) more useful to regard the substratum as
> impersonal. Moreover it w[oul] d be possible to produce
> effects without having any metaphysic whatever. . .
> (Quoted by Grover Smith, *Letters,* p. 406n.)

Huxley puts an emphasis on effect which has led Wyndham
Lewis some ten years earlier to see him in his acid way as a
"baser" variety of "Marcel Proust, in the same tradition" (*Time
and Western Man*).

VIII

ELIOT AND THE PARTICLE PHYSICIST

Do not let me hear
Of the wisdom of old men, but rather of their folly,
Their fear of fear and frenzy, their fear of possession,
Of belonging to another, or to others, or to God. . .

East Coker

We might as well acknowledge a certain tediousness as inevitable to such questions as the relation of the Self to the Other, the justification of awareness. A Prufrock is in some degree a burden to endure, and so too is Eliot or Whitehead or, for that matter, Augustine. One notices on occasion an impatience in Pound with Eliot, Pound choosing to solve the problem we are laboring as Parain says one must eventually solve it: "There remains then the Prince, he who simply asserts that language is the means of the mind which reveals itself thus, and so exercises its sovereignty. . . It has to be an act." Hence Pound's acceptance of the image as vortex in that revealing definition of image contained in his *Gaudier-Brzeska*. Image, he says, "is not an idea. It is a radiant node or cluster; it is what I can, and must perforce, call a VORTEX, from which and through which, and into which, ideas are constantly rushing." Hence also Pound's ideal of the Poet King to replace Plato's Philosopher King. Nor may we forget Pound's cavil on Guinicelli, whose words Eliot borrows out of Dante to use in his dedication of *The Waste Land* to Pound. Guido, Pound says in *The Spirit of Romance*, "introduced into romance poetry that new style in which the eyes and the heart and the soul have separate voices of their own and converse together." The development is of interest to literary technique, but it also inescapably contributes to a fragmentation through abstraction, turning poetry reflective. It is not the metamorphic mode Pound himself celebrates, acts out, in his own poetry, and we note that Pound's praise of Dante as supreme poet is largely for his having overcome the inherent dangers of the reflective, allegorical underpinnings of the *Divine Comedy* which grew out of the new style. Pound's position is rather clear from his remark that with Guido Guinicelli, "God became interesting, and speculation with open eyes and a rather didactic voice, is boon companion to the bard. Thought. . .now makes conquest of the matter of verse." Better Arnaut Daniel and the elegance of Circe's hair than Guinicelli and the mottoes on sun-dials. ("The sum of the charges against Daniel," Pound says at the outset of his career, "seems to be that he is difficult to read," a charge most constantly leveled against Pound, for the texture of his poetry, not for his meaning, as is the case with Eliot's concern with mottoes.)

If Pound's poetry turns outward from the concern for the relation of image to awareness—in the interest of larger social and political ends, in the interest of words as action—Eliot's rather turns inward upon that very concern, in the interest of being. One notes in him a *meticulousness* as a constant, in contrast to Pound. It is Pound who gives us problems with his text as text. We have little need of errata to Eliot's poems. And that meticulousness which exhibits itself on the surface runs deeper. It is *meticulousness* to which still cling some of the root meanings of the word: *timidity, fearfulness.* There is an extreme care exhibited for the detail, whether the choice of preposition ("Sweeney *among* the Nightingales") or of epigraphs. But to Eliot the care is finally necessary beyond its tediousness, since through it we are allowed to discover just how important the personal element of his poetry is to that poetry, as well as in what manner the personal is also universal. That such meticulous reflection may be of importance beyond our concerns for poetry itself is argued by Eliot in the *Four Quartets,* and in his latter essays, where in reflecting upon the earlier poetry he declares the poems did not mean what they seemed to mean at the time he wrote them.

The tedious argument of the relation of the self to the "out there," an argument capable of shifting with insidious intent when one isn't careful, may be abandoned, but at peril, as Pound was to discover in that political dedication to the Poet Prince which led him to the cage at Pisa. (I have developed this argument at some length in my *Ezra Pound: a Critical Essay.*) It can be more generally crucial as well. In the light of our agonies over the burdens modern science seems to have bequeathed us through the agency of "scientism"—the spectres of pollution and the bomb that disturb our sleep—we might for a moment consider the condition of modern physics, so radically changed from the days when Eliot's mentor Bertrand Russell engaged himself with confidence in physics's behalf. In the manner of the scientific mind at the turn of the century, Russell can put aside the problem of Husserl's "Original Intuition," and report with an amused pleasure, bordering on glee, that modern physics has more and more established Bishop Berkeley while trying to dislodge him. His delight seems over physics's discomfort, and not out of an interest in the consequences of that discomfort, for finally he lacks the serious interest that his nineteenth century counterpart, Thomas Henry Huxley, may be credited with.

The year before Eliot published *For Lancelot Andrewes: Essays on Style and Order* (1928), Werner Heisenberg propounded his "Principle of Uncertainty," which holds it impossible to determine both the position and the velocity of an electron at the same time. That is, the very act of observation affects its direction and speed. The more accurately its velocity is determined, the more indefinite its position. And in a cruious constancy which sets that effect outside the will of the observer, the mathematical margin of uncertainty in the measurement of place and velocity is always a function of Planck's constant, itself mysterious enough to give the reflective pause. Since Heisenberg's discovery in 1927, the neo-scholastic age of particle physics has occupied us increasingly because of its ramifications in philosophy and religion. Today physics, theology, philosophy find themselves interdependent again as they have not been since the late Middle Ages, and from the ancient debate of angels on pinheads, we have come to the serious metaphysical consideration of the photon. The photon's earlier theoretical rest mass was considered infinite in quantum electrodynamics; today we have come to a theoretical rest mass of zero for it. *Science News* reports that the old theory "was manifestly inappropriate, and a way was found to redo the mathematics so that the mass came out zero. The result doesn't quite satisfy everybody" (July 17, 1971). To have meaning, the infinitesimal particle has to relate to the whole of existence, to theory made real. Physicist Norman Kroll says on the point, "We really have no idea from the point of view of theoretical physics why the photon mass should be zero," and in summarizing the problem the editor of *Science News* concludes, "Behind it is no known profound philosophical reason," adding wistfully that "it may be just an accident." But accident won't quite do, as Wyndham Lewis's devastating insight into relativistic physics as expounded by Russell showed long ago: "the old romance and. . .inspiration of the hard-as-nuts, matter-of-fact, . . .weakest-go-to-the-wall, 'impersonal' attitude of the old-fashioned materialist. . .is still theirs. They [were] converts to a 'new materialism'. The bridge that we. . .witness Mr. Russell building. . .by means of the 'mathematical knowledge required'. . .over the gulf that separates the world of physics from the world of sense, is a very *material* bridge indeed. When you stand back and examine it from a distance, it looks like a business-like iron structure built between two clouds, with its girders thrust into the waves of an exceedingly deep ocean." The unknown "profound philosophical reason" of *Science News* reflects the physicist's uneasy feeling that we must turn back to metaphysics to discover again the truth of what Lewis said of the "conception of matter" in 1927 (his italics): *"It is art or metaphysics that is in question, rather than fact or natural science."*

The romance of the photon, as serialized in that fascinating periodical *Science News,* bears Lewis out. It comments on the paradox that threatens to entrap the theoretical physicist in his bridge building; as the postulated fragment of existence becomes smaller, the instrument of its pursuit in the natural world becomes larger, so that cloud chambers, spark chambers, neutrino observatories become larger than the tower of Babel. In pursuit of evidence of mass zero, Dr. William Park, a particle physicist, says, "If the mass really is zero, . . .it's one hell of a fine conspiracy," since it would mean that a zero rest mass for the photon is not an accident but that "the universe is put together in such a way that a photon cannot have a rest mass." It would mean, in other words, that existence is actively sustained, that the photon is not allowed to rest, and consequently that its movement cannot be explained as from within itself, any more than Whitehead answers the phenomenological problem by saying it is better to say feelings *aim at* entities rather than are *aimed at.*

If the idea of immanence is the modern philosophy (as opposed to the medieval idea of transcendence) in the neo-scholasticism of particle physics, we may be discovering the necessity of abandoning that idea to return to transcendence. Consider the question of the anti-particle, out of which particles emerge; one is very close to the edge of creation *ex nihilo* in such a conception of matter. The non-existent, which nevertheless has to be given name and negative qualities (and compare the scholastic difficulties with the definition of evil), becomes existent, so "short-lived" in that process as not to leave the track—the history—of its transformation from non-existence into existence in the enormous bubble chambers constructed to certify it. In the absence of *history,* the *myth* of theory sustains the search, through "a kind of mysticism among physicists about. . .constants" (*Science News*, May 13, 1972). So we come to the startling statement by an unnamed physicist that "God made the fine structure constant equal to 1/137 so that we would arise to worship Him."

The concern we have with particle physics in relation to Eliot does not require an understanding of the complexities of particle physics in its particularity, as fascinating to the mind as the subject is. We are interested to notice instead the obvious enlargement of sicentific and philosophical speculation and experimentation from Hartley's *ideas* as particles in the mind, through the new faith in a self-sustained, accidental universe of the late nineteenth and early twentieth centuries, to the loss of faith in immanence out of accident—whether immanence be looked at as the evolution of species or the burgeoning of an élan vital. We have come more and more, with less and less embarrassment to the scientist, to the role in physics and astronomy of what Eliot was to name (in *Little Gidding*) as the voice of that Calling. It is through an acceptance of that Calling that Eliot was himself to reach an accommodation of awareness to the "out there," and in doing so he may be said to have preceded the man of science as Wordsworth prophesies the modern poet's role to be.

There is even a parallel here, as I have already implied, between science and art in the role which *theory* and *myth* play in each. Eliot, in reviewing Joyce's *Ulysses*, for *The Dial* in 1923, declares that myth

> . . .is simply a way of controlling, of ordering, of giving a shape and a significance to the immense panorama of futility and anarchy which is contemporary history. . . .It is a method for which the horoscope is auspicious . . .Instead of the narrative method, we may now use the mythical method. It is, I seriously believe, a step toward making a modern world possible for art.

A way, but not a *simple* way; and Eliot's intellectual consent to myth as a *means* of ordering by the mind, *method* as a device under the control of the mind, proves insufficient. Myth becomes terrifyingly real as he discovers that its roots in the mind are nourished by something larger than human mind. The witty suggestion that the horoscope is auspicious for the method partakes of dramatic irony in the light of Eliot's later position and of the spectacular revival of astrology alongside astronomy since that statement. Theory, science's myth, which in the old days led to an investment of one's faith in accident, has begun to betray the scientist's intellectual consent. He finds himself engaged at a deeply personal level, where it is increasingly difficult to remain objective and impersonal, which indeed seems to require of the scientific mind in spite of itself a giving of the self which is

> A condition of complete simplicity
> (Costing not less than everything).

The ancient questions which we will increasingly contend with in spite of the surface spectacle of the community effect of recent science—from the Bomb to the new makeshift metaphysics of ecology—are and must be joined at a deeper level of the personal than any historical segment named "generation" will allow. Why something rather than nothing: a tree in nature, a particle in physics, a word on the lips? Awareness itself? To the degree that Eliot's poetry is an imitation of that inevitable personal engagement, it becomes more universal than the history of post-World War I London or the biographical facts of T. S. Eliot. Still, it *is* an engagement at the personal level, so that Eliot's history and our century's history cannot finally be disengaged from it. It is through such surfaces that we must descend deeper in order to reach the significant personal, even as Eliot himself admits a concern with what he called *"significant emotion"* in his essay seeking to define individual talent. With the question of the personal, we may return to Eliot and to the document of his sturggle in which he reflects upon it, *The Waste Land*.

IX

THE MEANING REVISED:
ESSAY AS AUTOBIOGRAPHY

I have said before
That the past experience revised in the meaning
Is not the experience of one life only
But of many generations. . .

Dry Salvages

In the midst of a lively and sometimes heated exchange of letters in the *Times Literary Supplement,* following the lead review of *The Waste Land* manuscript on December 10, 1971, the chairman of Faber and Faber, Peter Du Sautoy, expressed hope for a full-scale, authorized biography of Eliot, a prospect Eliot opposed. That failing, "there will certainly be a very full collection of letters published." The attitude toward the biographical problem in Eliot as expressed by some of the correspondents who suggest that Eliot had something sordid to hide rather widely misses the point of his reluctance to submit to a biography. For the point is that Eliot has already written what he considers to be his significant biography. That biography is in his essays, and most particularly in the *Selected Essays.* He calls it, in his prefatory note to the 1950 edition, "a kind of historical record of my interests and opinions." That is Eliot's way of saying, I think, that they contain what he considers the significant personal, the essential record of his deepest engagement of life. Where Thomas Hardy ghost-writes his own biography, in the name of his second wife, Eliot presents his in a more direct and yet more subtle way through his selection.

The difficulty a student of Eliot has in viewing the *Selected Essays* as biography lies partly in Eliot's progressive discovery of that aspect of them himself. The essays, read in this light, reveal a moment, one might say, from the essay as accidental biography to the essay as deliberate autobiography. One measures the difference in the distance between "Tradition and the Individual Talent" (1919) and his consideration of "The *Pensées* of Pascal" (1931). Not, of course, that Eliot lacks self awareness in the earlier prose; it is rather that he becomes more deeply aware in the later. From those early attempts at objective literary criticism he comes finally to the position where his own history is an intricate part of the criticism. He calls our attention to this point in "To Criticise the Critic" (1961):

> When I publish a collection of essays, or whenever
> I allow an essay to be re-published elsewhere, I make a

> point of indicating the original date of publication, as a
> reminder to the reader of the distance of time that sepa-
> rates the author when he wrote it from the author as he
> is today. . .the quotation of pronouncements of many
> years ago, as if they had been made yesterday, is. . .fre-
> quent.

The consequent distortion by such quotation out of the context
of time is a distortion of the significantly personal. One must
keep the point in mind in dealing with Eliot's remark in 1961
that "as for Classicism and Romanticism, I find that the terms
have no longer the importance to me that they once had." Remembering his earlier attack upon Wordsworth in the first piece
of the *Selected Essays,* we may be somewhat surprised to hear
him declare late in life (again in "To Criticise the Critic") that
"the nearest we get to pure literary criticism is the criticism
of artists writing about their own art; and for this I turn to Johnson, and Wordsworth and Coleridge." The statement is ac-
companied by the acknowledgment that in his early essays he
was engaged in defending the kind of poetry he and his friends
were writing, and what he values about them is the intensity of
the convictions, what he calls, in speaking of this quality in his
essay on Baudelaire, "a fundamental sincerity."

Nor is he oblivious to an arrogant innocence in them.
Increasingly after *The Waste Land* he finds himself embarrassed
by the popularity of such terms as "objective correlative" and
"dissociation of sensibility." For they are, seen in retrospect,
attempts to deal with personal concerns obliquely. Where he
had attempted earlier to set himself apart from the nineteenth
century romantic and associate his stance with that of the six-
teenth and seventeenth century poets, he now sees that as an
impossibility. For those early poets could assume that writing
poetry is a natural enough occupation of the mind and not
have to justify poetry either to themselves or to an audience.
In later years, with his own poetry behind him, Eliot reflects
upon the rise of such a remarkable critic as Samuel Johnson and
sees him a sign that something has been lost to the poet, an old
community of mind that made criticism less necessary than it
increasingly becomes in the eighteenth and nineteenth centuries.
For, though the rise of criticism may be seen as a cause of
poetry's decline (a charge the poet is fond of directing against
the critic) it seems equally tenable as an effect. The dislocation

of sensibilities involved a disolocation of the poet from society as well, a condition whose history Eliot inquires into. For he is no less interested in the history of ideas than in a "New Criticism" with which he has been historically associated as a founder.

During the eighteenth and nineteenth centuries, the poet becomes engrossed in, and increasingly obsessed by, his own perceptions and begins to lament and protest his isolation from the world about him, most particularly his separation from society, making of that separation a virtue if he is a Byron or Shelley. After all, the poet must "construct something/Upon which to rejoice." The seeds of discord are transplanted to English soil much earlier, of course. They are certainly in Sidney's "Apology," a discourse torn between refuting Plato's old charge against the poet as deceiver and certifying that charge. Perhaps such a divided mind about the poet is in the tension of *The Tempest,* delicate and bitter-sweet. It surely breaks into violent resolution with the Puritan closing of the ungodly theatre and in the baptized new Republic, New England; the sentiment against the users of words (unless they were directly anchored in the Word) flourished to such a degree that Thoreau apologizes for making notes. Hawthorne felt it necessary to adapt the preacher's devices of allegory and parable.

The man of letters finds himself in a difficult situation in his relation to society in England and America at the beginning of the nineteenth century. We may look briefly at an eighteenth-century thinker who contributes to those difficulties, since in his political philosophy he has much in common with Eliot, but little in aesthetic philosophy. Given his contributions to political debate in such of his works as *Reflections on the Revolution in France* and his speeches and letters on the American Revolution, one may be somewhat surprised by the "romantic" turn Edmund Burke's theory of aesthetics takes. It was written early in his career. Whether it was an influence of marked degree on subsequent aesthetic thought or more nearly a reflection of a climate of thought which itself was the influence, it nevertheless gives us some help in seeing a transition from Milton to Poe, from Doone to Whitman, for its implication shifts aesthetics from an anchor in transcendence to immanence. His *Philosophical Enquiry into the Origin of Our Ideas of the Sublime and Beautiful* (1757) is in defense of God by intention, as was

Bishop Berkeley's *Treatise Concerning the Principles of Human Knowledge* some fifty years earlier, but the advocacy of neither effects that intention. Burke's treatise, indeed, was an attempt to recover from the dislocation of Berkeley's arguments, so that a relationship could be established between the knower and the external world once more. The external world, in the argument, gains a new authority as God's signature to man, through which man is returned to a proper piety in relation to both God and the natural world. But because of the emphasis upon the *knower* in Burke's argument, the "origin" of the ideas of the sublime and beautiful begins to look suspiciously resident in the knower, and particularly so if one is inclined to disfranchise God from the scheme of things, as nineteenth century thought increasingly was.

The most significant contribution of Burke's essay seems his deliberate examination of the psychological effects of terror and pain upon his own sensibility. He rejects the Neo-Classical and New Science approaches to the problem, except insofar as they may be of subordinate use to him. Or rather, he does not accept them as positions from which to examine the problem, choosing rather to examine aesthetic experience as close to the personal and as far from the theoretical as possible. He is interested in the subjective emotional effect of objects apprehended by the senses, and his examination of the problem echoes Stephen Dedalus's severe subjection of the senses in Chapter IV of *The Portrait of the Artist as a Young Man,* except that Burke wishes to elevate the senses to a new dignity, as Stephen does not. It is in defense of the senses that he writes, as Wordsworth is to do in his modification of Plato in "Tintern Abbey." For in that poem, it is the senses that gently lead one into a restful union with nature, not as in Plato, where the mind alone is sufficient to a rest transcending nature and the senses. In Plato's argument, beauty is healing. Pleasure is the absence of pain. Pain and ugliness are absences whose immediate "objective correlative" is the world of the shadow, nature. The natural world, then, including the body, is a negation, not to be trusted by the mind. But in Burke's argument, pain and terror have positive effect; it is directly through them that one wins transcendence. (And in this respect, we might well make the argument that Burke is in a sense a forerunner of Baudelaire.)

For Burke, *terror* in the emotions, through a response to

the external world, is an effect ultimately of the sublime. It is to be described at its highest emotional point as *astonishment*, with subordinate emotional degrees of *awe, reverence, respect*. He is concerned with the intended effects of the graveyard poets and the gothic novelists, with rescuing them from the Puritan charge of pandering to frivolous and indolent emotional indulgences. Astonishment is "that state of soul in which all its motions are suspended with some degree of horror." It is nevertheless "a sort of delightful horror, a sort of tranquillity tinged with terror." And in that last phrase we have anticipation of Wordsworth's preoccupation with the mind's astonishment in nature, as in his definition of poetry as emotion recollected in tranquillity. Compare, for instance, his recollections of the terror he felt as a child at the huge presence of nature in "The Prelude" and the calm and tranquil expression of "Tintern Abbey," a poem which is nevertheless touched with a tinge of terror. Emotion to Burke is an extension of sensation, from which we derive our ideas of the sublime, such ideas as we express in terms like *obscurity, power, privations, vastness, infinity, difficulty, magnificence*.

But the classical concern for precision, purity, order are suspect, especially as they may be discovered in the new philosophy out of Descartes, leading to the mechanist thought of Locke and Hartley. So when Descartes declares that "all things that I know clearly and distinctly are true," Burke responds, "A clear idea is. . .another name for a little idea." Burke's concern for piety requires a subordination of the finite knower, but his emphasis nevertheless gives an authority to that finite knower which can and will be read as further evidence that the knower is the cause of his world. He is somewhere between the Hulme-Locke-Hartley explications of the mind as a sort of passive computer and the solipsistic explicators of the mind as the cause of its private and only world. But his argument is bearing toward the aesthetics of Wallace Stevens, given its emphasis upon the authority of emotion. His treatise is a step toward the elevation of feeling over thought, to which our century has, in respect to literature, attached the term Victorianism and, for its American manifestation, Transcendentalism.

We know Eliot's reaction to Emerson and Tennyson and Arnold, seeing them as he does initially in the historical perspective of his "dissociation of sensibility," that separation of

thought and feeling that is the particular hell of J. Alfred Prufrock. And we know his interest in Poe and Baudelaire as anti-
thetical. Poe, the renegade, in substance turns Burke's sublime
inside out. It is well enough to assume that sublimity depends
upon qualities resident in the object, the perception of which
makes the perceiver painfully aware of his own insufficiency.
Thus, if the ultimate sublime is God, then the great ruins of
antiquity certify his grandeur by terror in the heart of the be-
holder. A disastrous flood, Burke holds, "turns the soul in upon
itself." Through the poet's refined response to nature—to ruins
and disasters—piety is rescued for mankind by art itself, and
Plato and the Puritans answered in their old charge. But Poe
presents a shocking alternative. His "Fall of the House of Usher"
casts, in its eerie light, not an image of a great decaying house
through which image one reflects upon the vanity of human
wishes, but the process of degeneration of mind into the Void.
Poe's grotesque echoes Burke's sublime in a most disturbingly
negative way.

Eliot can, in retrospect, see in himself the romantic's uneasy version of the poet in society. He can appreciate more
fully, because of his own struggle, Coleridge's attempt to bring
the poet back into society by enlisting poetry in the service of
the great I AM in his famous discourse on the fancy and imagination. He can see also the burden of those New England Puritan
suspicions of the artist which he carried to England with him
when he thought he was leaving them behind. That burden
emerges in his critical concern with Hawthorne, Poe, James, on
whom he writes repeatedly, and it does not depend for our
notice upon the biographical facts of his mother's disappointment that he would give up a professorship in philosophy for vers
libre or of his father's restriction upon his inheritance as a
punishment for his accepting that calling, though that surface
evidence is comfortable enough to deal with. Eliot struggled to
come to terms with letters in a personal way and, given the victory, achieve for the poet a station of high accord in an enlightened society. When he declares himself a Royalist, Tory,
Anglican, he asserts a position in the name of those exiled
romantics who pursued such a role—such writers as James and
Wordsworth and Coleridge. (Is Wordsworth or Coleridge any
less "realist" than James?)

Certain of the later essays are rather openly and explicitly intended to point to what Eliot considers the relevant biography of himself as poet, the history of the intellectual and spiritual development which he looks back upon. "To Criticise the Critic" is, as we have noticed, an obvious instance. So also, in the *Selected Essays,* such pieces as "Thoughts after Lambeth" (1931) and his thoughts about humanism (1927-28). In those we may witness Eliot coming to a conception of a desirable approach to the poet and his work through critical biography, a conception Croce argues as the proper role of the monograph:

> Monographs on poets attain their end when they are not merely collections of scattered observations or aesthetic comments on single works, but when they succeed in giving the characteristic quality of the motive or fundamental state of mind of the poet, and in some way correct and enrich what we already possess on the subject.

But there are others of the essays which are less direct but more consciously autobiographical, essays examining individual poets and critics who allow Eliot an intensive examination of the personal without the intrusion of the historical or of the testimonial. They are essays in which we encounter a double portrait, one of which is Eliot's, consciously drawn and as consciously hidden from the eyes of the merely curious. To read such essays in this light is to experience a set of Plutarchian lives, one of them buried like the hidden term of a metaphor. An obvious example of the type is "The *Pensées* of Pascal" (1931). A more interesting example, in the light of the fascination with the possibly scandalous side of Eliot's life which floats through the letters exchanged in the *Times Literary Supplement,* is his "Baudelaire" (1930). In it, Eliot anticipates precisely those confusions that Professor G. Wilson Knight perpetuates in the letters column of the *TLS.* The Pascal essay we may defer for the moment.

X

THE TROUBLESOME HYACINTH GIRL

In order to arrive at what you do not know
  You must go by a way which is the way of ignorance.

East Coker

In quoting passages from Eliot's portrait of Fresca, the reviewer for the *Times Literary Supplement* concludes: "These passages make it plain that those readers, from I. A. Richards to Randall Jarrell and beyond, who have seen the emotional impetus behind *The Waste Land* as hatred and fear of sex, will find their suspicions confirmed more completely than they could have hoped." G. Wilson Knight introduces again the argument that the loss reflected in *The Waste Land* has its cause in the death of Eliot's friend Jean Verdenal, to whom *Prufrock and Other Observations* is dedicated. The debate which ensued centered around the lines of "The Burial of the Dead" in which one sees the hyacinth girl, arms full of flowers, followed by the lines echoed out of *The Tempest,* "Those are pearls that were his eyes." But it is a debate which does not take into account either the technical complexities of Eliot's point of view or the intellectual complexities of what he is attempting in the poem. "His" eyes? Why "his"? ". . .I am happy to agree with Professor G. Wilson Knight (January 28) that the 'key' to *The Waste Land* is to be found in the mystical experience of the Hyacinth garden followed by a cry of desolation so poignant that it has to be expressed in another language," writes Peter Dunn (*TLS*, February 11, 1972), quoting a phrase from Eliot about the human experience of having "had the experience but missed the meaning." But that the desolation requires a foreign language may not be so much the point as the source of the foreign phrase, from Wagner's *Tristan,* one of the oldest of those romantic treatments of love such as Dante shows to relegate one to hell. Empty and waste the sea of such love, and the experience is poignant not because it reflects a "mystical experience," but rather an experience in which all mystery is denied. We are surely in the region of Paolo and Francesca, and Professor Knight in returning to the argument by calling our attention again to a reading of *The Waste Land* as an elegy to some lost male, citing the word *brother* from the fragments, remains rather wide of the mark.

The controversy is complicated meanwhile by a very inadequate book called *T. S. Eliot: a Memoir,* by Robert Sencourt (New York: Dodd, Mead, 1971), in which Sencourt manages both to deny and affirm Eliot's mysticism. In the interest of his own participation in Eliot's conversion to Anglo-Catholicism, he fails to give sufficient weight to Eliot's earlier spiritual quest, prior to 1927 when he met Eliot. (Less than half the book is memoir, the rest being an accounting of Eliot's life up to 1927, largely from secondary sources.) Sencourt's skating on the edge of scandal in respect to Eliot's unhappy first marriage leads Eliot's friend J. Chiari (*TLS,* December 31, 1971) to record that "Robert Sencourt came to see me three times when I lived in Southampton, and he was among those who were and perhaps still are obsessed with the notion of homosexuality."

In spite of their good sense, neither Dame Helen Gardner nor Anne Riddler satisfies the relentless pursuers of Hyacinthus in Eliot's poetry, so that two months later, Chiari enters the debate again in Eliot's defense. "The Hyacinth girl of 'The Burial of the Dead'. . .conveys an experience of man-woman love so absolutely fulfilled as to reach the mystical and the ineffable. The hyacinth in Eliot's poetry is always associated with dreams of love, memories of past or unattained happy moments, and has nothing to do with the Hyacinth boy of Apollo." Chiari is the most intelligent of the commentators in this exchange, but he too misses the vital point here, as Dunn has done before him. The poignancy is not a result of a mystical experience which falls away in desolation, nor of a fulfillment reaching the mystical and ineffable. The despair in the passage is that no mystical experience occurs through the encounter. The point seems rather that the "male" of the pair has gone as far with worldly love as possible, but regardless of the fulfilled desire there is yet a desire unfulfilled. He is left looking into the heart of silence, with opaque eyes, eyes that are at best reflectors such as a Narcissus might possess. The reading that would unravel the puzzle should begin not with Hyacinthus but with Narcissus. The failure and despair is the same as we have discovered in the "Preludes," in "Portrait of a Lady," and in "La Figlia che Piange." Irritation and anger no doubt prevent Chiari from making the point, for it is implicit in his concluding statement that "Eliot had to go beyond despair and 'The Hollow Men' to 'Ash Wednesday,' or commit suicide." It remains only to be said of Chiari's last sentence that in the spiritual journey Eliot makes, the state of *The Waste Land* is preceded by that of "The Hollow

Men," though the latter poem follows in the chronology of publication. For "The Hollow Men" records a glazed existence of opaque eyes, eyes which cannot see through to eyes or any light beyond their own reflection off broken columns. As we shall presently see more clearly, the progress in *The Waste Land* as an account of salvation goes beyond that point of despair which "The Hollow Men" records.

As for Eliot's supposed hatred of women, or the sordidness of sex, such as that recorded in the typist scene, we have reached too easy a conclusion when we establish the cause in Eliot's own unhappy life with Vivien. In his analysis of that "fragmentary Dante," Baudelaire, he attempts to set such misunderstanding to rights. Baudelaire's

> human love is definite and positive, his divine love vague and uncertain: hence his insistence upon the evil of love, hence his constant vituperations of the female. In this there is no need to pry for psychopathological causes, which would be irrelevant at best; for his attitude towards women in consistent with the point of view which he had reached. . . He has arrived at the perception that a woman must be to some extent a symbol; he did not arrive at the point of harmonising his experience with his ideal needs.

And Baudelaire did not arrive at that point of harmony precisely because he was struggling from the dark side of life and through it in a half blind way. In such reminders to us of the unnecessary prying into psychopathology and of Baudelaire's realization of woman as "to some extent symbol," Eliot is surely speaking to us about himself. He speaks also of the personal in the statement that Baudelaire "is discovering Christianity for himself; he is not assuming it as a fashion or weighing social or political reasons, or any other accidents. He is beginning, in a way, at the beginning, and being a discoverer, is not altogether certain what he is exploring and to what it leads; he might almost be said to be making again, as one man, the effort of scores of generations."

Is Eliot, as a student comments on *The Waste Land*, presenting "a very unromantic picture" of love? It is rather that he presents an excessively romantic picture of love, pushing romanticism to its depths, even as he sees Baudelaire doing. For if we

take romanticism in one of its aspects as a vague, sympathetic
inclination to an image or object, the end must be that our
feelings are forced to curl about such an image or object. The
"other" can be but mirror to us. To intensify that inclination by
a vague, negative sympathy, furiously pursued as Baudelaire
does, is to arrive at a perception of the symbol as the threshold
through which one sees the dark side of romanticism. It is the
romantic approach of Baudelaire and Rimbaud and Charles-
Louis Philippe (whose *Bubu de Montparnasse* is one of the
myriad sources for the "sordid" details of *The Waste Land*).
"For Baudelaire," says Eliot, "sexual operation is at least something not analogous to Kruschen Salts," as it is taken to be in the
Freudian concerns that lead to one's prying into "psychopatho-
logical causes."

　　Not that Eliot hasn't been given to such simplifications
in his youth. The enthusiastic letter he writes Russell in appreciation of Russell's therapeutic visit to the country with Vivien
in 1916 has that quality about it. Eliot is prepared to credit the
saving of Vivien's life to Russell's "sensitivity" session with her.
It is an approach one might expect of a liberalized unitarian
such as the young Eliot, which position he sees in a very different light by 1928. Writing on Freud's *The Future of an Illusion*, he is scathing in his attack upon the "parvenue" science
of psychology, and finds its most celebrated practitioner guilty
of a "stupidity" which "appears not so much in historical ignorance or lack of sympathy with the religious attitude [both fail-
ings of Freud also], as in verbal vagueness and inability to reason." In this book on the future of religion, Freud has given a
highly inadequate definition of culture, which Eliot dismembers
effectively. By this point in his own development (1928), he is
remembering his early encounter with Dante and seeing in him a
fuller expression of the individual's relation to community, in-
volving the whole being. And he can see, as his essay on "Baudelaire" makes clear, that when sex is reduced to the role of thera-
py or cathartic, neither sex nor sin is taken as seriously as they
require. The extensions of that failure have become a major
element in the decay of civilization. The error of Freud's attempt at what he calls "the preservation of mankind against
nature," in which argument neither *nature* nor *man* is given
adequate definition, leads us, for instance, to our current enlargement from the individual to the mass scale in the rage for
the sensitivity session, which is a kind of extension of unitarian-

ism to its illogical extreme. The deeper implications of the obscene, such as those inherent in Greek tragedy, are discarded, and the significant personal is lost in the death of manners, as if manners were simply conventions, expendable as yesterday's newspaper. Manners are, at their best, those gestures of deference to whatever is not myself, the practice of which on occasion strengthens one to the point where he may love that which is not the self. The alternative to manners as a mode of address to the other, through which one may express a reverence for existences other than the self, is the world of the jungle, where *life* can mean only *life force,* with a one-dimensional meaning to life. The emotional orgy, whether Freudian analysis under semi-private conditions or mass sessions, may appear to us in the future as being more blindly destructive than the medieval barber's letting of blood appears to us today. Eliot refines his concern with this problem of psychology's role in the soul's health in *The Cocktail Party.* He presented the problem more startlingly in that picturing of unitarian Bacchantes dismembering Bertrand Russell at the Boston cocktail party of "Mr. Apollinax" than he could have known at the time.

Eliot's early enthusiasm with the poet Dante becomes considerably more. It helps prepare him to see that "in the adjustment of the natural to the spiritual, of the bestial to the human and the human to the supernatural, Baudelaire is a bungler compared with Dante." One might indeed say that in *The Waste Land* it is Baudelaire as bungler who is dramatized in the journey. It is to Baudelaire that Eliot traces the origin of the "poetry of flight," specifically to a passage in the prose *Journaux Intimes,* those secret reflections on the quest. And again, as if speaking to those who have ears to hear the personal, Eliot says of his interest in this prose work:

> It must not be forgotten that a poet in a romantic *age* cannot be a 'classical' poet except in tendency. . . .For such poets we may expect often to get much help from reading their prose works and even notes and diaries; help in diciphering the discrepancies between head and heart, means and end, material and ideals.

There can be little doubt in Eliot's mind in 1931, as these remarks reflect, that his own is the romantic heart, the classical head. It is the classical head which makes him see the necessity of a mirror behind the mirror of awareness in nature if a more complete picture of the human quest is to be reflected by art. He has already practiced the idea through technique in lesser poems. There is his use of that medieval tapestry reflecting pagan myth as read by a romantic, one-color mind in the epigraph to "Sweeney Erect." And Sweeney is presented as one of the ends which dissociated sensibility reaches, as Prufrock is another.

If the heart of Baudelaire, with all the discomforts of its dark side, is so much a part of the texture of *The Waste Land,* the head of Dante is there too, infused and not so obvious. That is, the way possible to the romantic through his intense and almost insane pursuit of the immediate has its complement in the greater poet. Jeanne Duval or Vivien Eliot provide images for one aspect of woman as symbol: Beatrice provides another. "The complement and correction to *Journaux Intimes,*" says Eliot," so far as they deal with the relations of man and woman, is the *Vita Nuova* and the *Divine Comedy.*" It is a corrective which allows one to see in Baudelaire's "Le Balcon" "all the romantic idea of Love, but something more: the reaching out towards something which cannot be had *in*, but which may be had partly through, personal relations. Indeed, in much romantic poetry the sadness is due to the exploitation of the fact that no human relations are adequate to human desires, but also to the disbelief in any further object for human desires than that which, being human, fails to satisfy them. One of the unhappy necessities of human experience is that we have to 'find things out for ourselves.' " No further *object* for human desires than those which have already failed that desire. In other words, we are on that threshold where the romantic turns classicist and at the point where a light other than wordly or intellectual desire becomes necessary, a point where eyes and the objects of those eyes become translucent so that one is about to see *through*, not simply *in*. Thus we have a statement by Eliot in his essay on Baudelaire that anticipates the possibility of one's seeing that

> the end of all our exploring
> Will be to arrive where we started
> And know the place for the first time.

The images and objects will not have changed, but the seeing will have, and consequently images and objects will be no longer mirrors for self-reflection but centers for the burning of a light deeply interfused in nature, including the beholding mind itself. At that point, even Priapus, "Whose flute is breathless," may be seen in a Keatsean richness of the sensual without that uneasiness one notices in the early Eliot. But that time is not yet, insofar as *The Waste Land*'s composition is concerned, though there are intimations of the possibility.

There is, for instance, the discarded "Elegy" which forms a part of *The Waste Land* manuscript. It is a nightmare out of "The Fall of the House of Ushers," and it seems somehow to partake of a riddle vision.

> I saw sepulchral gates flung wide,
> Reveal (as in a tale by Poe)
> The features of the injured bride!
>
> That hand, prophetical and slow
> (Once warm, once lovely, often kissed)
> Tore the disordered cerements,
> Around the head the scorpions hissed!

We are in the presence of a wronged Aspatia, and no unbounded remorse or intesne grief can "expiate the fault." The guilt is overwhelming and terrifying, but it is not a guilt to be explained as sexual, such as have made Poe a rich fund for psychological plunderings. For Eliot's poem turns from Poe to Thompson. The poet of flight finds himself quarry to the Hound of Heaven.

> God, in a rolling ball of fire
> Pursues by day my errant feet.
> His flames of anger and desire
> Approach me with consuming heat.

The poetry is not persuasive enough for the "Elegy" to figure helpfully in *The Waste Land*. For one thing, it is told from outside the experience, a report whose reflective evaluation lacks the intensity of Poe's or Baudelaire's surrealistic representations of the terror of pursuit. It is too much a display of the weakness of form Eliot speculates about when he hazards that "the conjecture that the care for perfection of form, among some of the romantics of the nineteenth century, was an effort to support, or to conceal from view, an inner disorder." (One thinks of Shelley's "Ode to the West Wind" and its terza rima at once.) What is needed is not a supporting or hiding of disorder, but a revealing and exorcising of it, which surrealism promised fair to answer.

Surrealism must not be artificial, as in Huysmans, presenting the chimera of the personal. It must carry that "fundatmental sincerity" of a Baudelaire which bears witness to a concern "with the real problem of good and evil." Startling juxtapositions, fused images, such as in Baudelaire's sudden focus upon the seething maggots in "Carrion" which give an illusion of life to the dead carcass; or upon the intimate mingling of light and sound and life in the cold crystals of "Jewels." Surrealism, after Baudelaire, becomes on occasion a device for summoning pathos to underline aloneness with a poignancy that promises revelation, as if through such a language beyond logic one were given a clue, the unriddling of which will dissolve surrealism into a new realism, mystery into revelation. It is the quality which gives to Poe the suggestion of an allegory whose center is never sufficiently revealed to allow the suggestiveness much deciphering beyond a faint surmise. But neither the arrogant boldness of surrealism as it progresses into Dada or the mechanical appropriation of the device as one encounters it in the poetry of revolt in the 1960s should obscure from us that Eliot in his surrealistic *Waste Land* is pursuing what Baudelaire discovered, that "what really matters in Sin and redemption," through which the bride may be discovered less horrible, the Thames less polluted, the world of the Unreal City less unreal.

The *TLS* reviewer, in defending his initial review of the manuscript, remarks, ". . .it would certainly be relevant to our understanding of *The Waste Land* to know if its author had ever experienced halluncination." We have seen that Bertrand Russell takes credit for having supplied such an experience for that dissolving mind Eliot dramatizes in his poem. In the second volume of his *Autobiography* Russell recalls London during World War I: "I used to have strange visions of London as a place of unreality. I used in imagination [i.e., he wills into experience] to see bridges collapse and sink, and the whole great city vanish like a morning mist. Its inhabitants began to seem like hallucinations, and I would wonder whether the world in which I thought I had lived was a mere product of my febrile nightmares." To the passage he appends the note, "I spoke of this to T. S. Eliot, who put it in *The Waste Land*." The note suggests that Russell did not so much recover from such nightmares as recast the mood of them with his more characteristic arrogance. The experience is already in Eliot's memory, as we see in earlier poems, nor is it unique to Eliot or Russell, being one of those common and ancient experiences of the mind out of which Plato wrestles the world as shadow and Augustine treats the city of man to the light of the city of God. Russell's evaluation of Eliot's character is in *Dear Bertrand Russell: A Selection of His Correspondence with the General Public: 1950-1968*. What Eliot would surely say to Russell's claim and to the reviewer's pondering appeal is that any one-dimensional view of the "other" is hallucinatory, no matter how persuasively one may cloak illusion with Renaissance art or drama, or with humanist thought out of the eighteenth century. Eyes of pearl may seem to be substantial and real in a material world, but they appear opaque in the wider and deeper vision. Until one truly "sees," there can be no double vision through which awareness can come to terms with its objects, and see beyond and through those objects to a cause that certifies its own existence as it cannot for itself. That is the point of return to the starting place, where the world can be accepted. It is the point also where, as Eliot will say later, one realizes that if the temple is to be destroyed, one must be forever rebuilding it that it may be destroyed. In that focused vision lies the accommodation of the unreal to the real city.

But, then, as we have said, that time is not yet. Dante lies teasingly behind and in and around *The Waste Land*, not so fully accepted by the heart as by the head. The heart is still largely like Baudelaire's, set on "discovering Christianity" for itself.

XI

THROUGH A GLASS DARKLY

In the middle, not only in the middle of the way
But all the way, in a dark wood, in a bramble,
On the edge of a grimpen, where is no secure foothold.

East Coker

The Waste Land is certainly a desperate poem, but not one in which desperation is insurmountable, if it is true (independent of the mind's recognition of the truth) that "the poetry of flight . . .is. . .a dim recognition of the direction of beatitude." These are Eliot's words in tribute to Baudelaire's desperation, for if Baudelaire exploited his weakness, "it was a way to liberate his mind." Eliot learned from Baudelaire to take suffering seriously, as he learned from Bradley to take the problem of awareness seriously. It is a lesson more important at the level of the significant personal than the one learned from Laforgue, whose presence is more obvious in Eliot's manner up to *The Waste Land*. By the time of *The Waste Land* the concern is more deeply with the spiritual implications of the empty and sordid "out there," filtering through into a consciousness that drifts as it suspends the fragments reflectively. That is, the consciousness suspends the fragments between the dual tensions of memory and desire. It is a consciousness captive to time and slowly realizing the desperateness of that captivity. The poem is not, as drama, tragic; or at best it is of that lesser tragic mode Aristotle distinguishes as the drama of suffering. Eliot sees this parallel in Baudelaire also, in whom there is a great strength, he says, "but strength merely to *suffer*. He could not escape suffering and could not transcend it, so he attracted pain to himself." If we wonder that Eliot could so radically revise his estimate of a romantic such as Wordsworth, the point from which to trace his change lies here in Baudelaire. Baudelaire is "the first counter-romantic in poetry." But so too is Wordsworth a "counter-romantic"; so too is any mind committed to reconciling the head and the heart. Eliot is such a mind himself, and comes to see that in Wordsworth's poetry of flight there is also the dim recognition of beatitude, less morbid and in its outcome more promising than Baudelaire's flight. Both poets, of course, turn inward. The suffering which Baudelaire attracts to himself is in Wordsworth turned outward from a freer spirit. If we are not convinced of Wordsworth's vision when he declares himself to have learned to look on nature in such a way as to hear in it "the still, sad music of humanity"—to have found in nature a spiritual

correlative for those inland murmurs that trouble him—we feel
at least that we are in the presence of a mind willing to give and
sympathize, working manfully with the head in the heart's interest in an attempt to control.

So Eliot will decalre a new esteem for Wordsworth, in *The
Use of Poetry and the Uses of Criticism;* and in "To Criticise the
Critic" he will cite Wordsworth and Coleridge (along with John-
son) as instances in whom we get the nearest "to pure literary
criticism." In the same essay he will declare that the terms
classical and romantic no longer engage him as they once did. He
has come to consider that if Baudelaire and Pascal have made
Dante accessible to him—as Dante was not in those days of the
"Preludes" when Eliot first read him, so have Wordsworth and
Coleridge helped him to see Dante as a complement to the dark
side of romanticism. Purgatory is a region possible now. Saint
Narcissus, "struck down by. . .knowledge" of the body's pre-
scribing the reaches of the eye's world, can "come out to live
under the rock." As desolate as is that region where two dreams
cross, on the threshold of a painful ascent of the mountain, there
is yet the possibility of a larger world. We hover in the region of
the late repentant, the hopeful exiles, in the first sections of
The Waste Land, as a prelude to striking out in flight once more.
But the new flight will be upward to an encounter with the
spirits of Arnaut and Guinicelli very near the summit. That encounter will be in "Ash-Wednesday," for those dying with "a
little patience" in *The Waste Land* are only just past "the agony
in the stony places" in the opening lines of "What the Thunder
Said" (lines we may profitably read with Canto IV of *Il Purgatorio* as background). Under the "red rock," where one waits
acceptance to the agonies of purgation, *rock* itself moves from
sign to symbol, from image to metaphor. Sterile rock with the
grace of rain makes possible the garden. But it is that grace
which makes one sweat not remain dry, which makes thought
no longer dry though in a dry and windy season. "If there were
rock/And also water" is prelude to the encounter on the road
to Emmaus which follows; and if it is on Peter, the rock, that
Christ first declares his Church to rest, in the rescue of time—if
time be constantly redeemed—each mind must in turn be that
burgeoning rock. We are anticipating ourselves; we have moved
beyond Tiresias and must return to his problem yet awhile.
In doing so we shall notice a blindness, an incompleteness, in
that seer not unlike a blindness in Eliot through which he strug-

gles with a personal agony that left him unable to speak—to write—for a time and made him fearful of his own mind. The issuance from silence is *The Waste Land,* in which there begins to dawn upon him a suspicion that his blindness is not bequeathed him so much by romantics such as Wordsworth, as by an intervening generation. Responsibility for distorting the terms romantic and classical he is now prepared to lay at the feet of Arnold and Pater.

XII

PAST ARNOLD AND PATER

If I think, again, of this place,
And of people, not wholly commendable,
Of no immediate kin or kindness,
But some of peculiar genius,
All touched by a common genius,
United in the strife which divided them. . .

Little Gidding

When one examines a poet or critic who is resolutely opposed to didacticism in art, what he is likely to discover is that the opposition is not to didacticism itself but to the particular message, the particular content, of the particular didactic art under attack. Pound sees Eliot as didactic from time to time, but it is difficult to think of a more didactic poet than Pound. What one then comes to is the question of how artful a poet's didacticism is, once we agree that art by its nature is an assertion to which the artist's mind ascribes validity by the very act of assertion. There may be poets dedicated to art for art's sake, but if so we never hear or know of them except by accident. For they do not publish their poems. When Tony Harrison writes "On Not Being Milton," he begins his poem

> Read and committed to the flames, I call these sixteen
> lines that go back to my roots my *cahier d'un retour au*
> *pays natal.*

But they are not committed to the flames: they are published in the *Times Literary Supplement* and circulated by the tens of thousands around the world. And still it may be argued that even such a completely private act as literally burning the lines is nevertheless an assertion, a publication to the self at least. Even Prufrock cannot refrain from an interest in the ordering of forms within his own mind, nor resist the temptation of addressing an audience, the ambiguous and buried "you." Art for art's sake, then, is a pose. Nor can the *poete maudit* escape the dilemma by assuming the air of the dandy. The concern for an initiated audience to which to play is quite often a way of playing to a much larger audience, which one studiedly attempts to shock. (A mark of a successful reaching into that audience in our day is the frequency with which one encounters the poet in the gossip columns of newspapers and magazines.)

In spite of the extreme circumstances of near poverty and a disturbing marraige, there remains a bit of the dandy about the early Eliot. It is hinted at in his clever yoking of Villon and

Heraclitus in Bertrand Russell's seminar. The atmosphere of languid, ironic wit is a part of the general climate the poet and would-be poet breathe at the turn of the century, a current from the Pre-Raphaelites and Pater, transmitted through the decadent nineties. That attitude stands one in good stead in the *Harvard Advocate* no less than in such literary salons as Lady Ottoline's, where the spirit of the Rhymers Club meets and mingles with the Bloombury circle. Bertrand Russell publishes a picture of himself walking with Lady Ottoline and Lytton Strachy "After the £ 100 fine" exacted at his trial for pacifist activism, an episode which in his recollection of it bears some of the flamboyant daring of Oscar Wilde during his trial. Pound is initially attracted to this region himself, and the seeming liveliness in the arts under such influences accounts somewhat for his insistence at the time that London is the literary capital of the world. He records the shocked anger resulting from the lifting of the veils. In Section XII of Hugh Selwyn Mauberly, there is a caricature of Lady Ottoline in "The Lady Valentine" (the clue is in the rhyme) for whom poetry is the border of ideas,

> The edge, uncertain, but a means of blending
> With other strata
> Where the lower and higher have ending;
>
> A hook to catch the Lady Jane's attention,
> A modulation toward the theatre,
> Also, in case of revolution,
> A possible friend and comforter.

But in spite of its hollowness there was an engaging style to be caught out of that tradition. One has only to compare Pater's didactic novel in defense of paganism to Newman's novel in defense of Christianity, *Marius the Eipcurean* to *Callista: a Sketch of the Third Century*. They have equivalent setting and time; they reflect the same point of crisis in Western Civlization, and yet Newman's is unbelievably dull by contrast. Pater's defining of Cyrenaicism through his own style suspends the present moment between the "hypothetical eternities" of past and future. It engages the troublesome problem of phenomenology through historical materials, and so suggests by its art that every moment of awareness which art suspends is a "Six o'clock," more gaudy than Eliot's. Through the suspension of the moment in words, the "burnt-out ends of smoky days" seems more palatable in Pater than Newman's refutation of that position.

Nor does Newman seem more persuasive in his handling of orthodoxy in poetry. He enlarges upon Satan's cry to the modern world that the mind is its own place:

> Each mind is its own centre, and it draws
> Home to itself, and moulds in its thoughts span
> All outward things, the vassals of its will,
> Aided by Heaven, by earth unthwarted still.

This argument on the relation of "Substance and Shadow" bears a didactic message whose complexities require the formal discursiveness one encounters more persuasively in *Apologia pro Vita Sua*. What one is most convinced of, and retains from the reading, is that this is bad poetry. Newman does not fare much better in his *Dream of Gerontius,* which takes the full grown soul on a journey to the seat of judgment. The poem is nevertheless suggestive of technical problems Eliot is to attempt solution for in his own "Gerontion." The Dantesquean flight into the transcendent is less possible to art since the eighteenth century than it was to Dante, for the movement into another dimension requires a more persuasive anchor in time to gain our consent since Dante's time. It is a point Eliot specifically makes in his writings on Dante, and it is a point he dramatizes by setting his journey of the mind firmly in the present historical moment of automobile traffic, pavement, lost golf balls, and picnic debris along the Thames.

One is less likely, then, to be convinced of a reality in the condition of the soul when it is made to rise to the bar of justice in Newman's handling of it. On the other hand, a drifting awareness in the world of nature gains a certain authority from naturalistic psychology. Newman's soul asks "Am I alive or dead?" It is in a state in which silence

> drives back my thoughts upon their spring
> By a strange introversion, and perforce
> I now begin to feed upon myself,
> Because I have nought else to feed upon.

It is a condition Eliot will echo in celebrating a state of spiritual emptiness, following an acceptance of self-failure and a renunciation, in "Ash-Wednesday":

> Because I cannot hope to turn again
> Consequently I rejoice, having to construct something
> Upon which to rejoice.

What Newman sees, Eliot will declare valid; *how* he presents it in fiction or poetry seems pale in comparison to such writers as Pater and Eliot himself. But Eliot nevertheless rescues something of what Newman attempts in his *Dream of Gerontius,* in his own "Gerontion" and in *The Waste Land.* Newman has the Gerontius's soul explain its strange sensations:

> A disembodied soul, thou hast by right
> No converse with aught else beside thyself;
> But, lest so stern a solitude should load
> And break thy being, in mercy are vouchsaf'd
> Some lower measures of perception
> [seemingly through the senses] ; symbols
> And not sensations, using "similitudes of earth."

Drama in a saved soul is hardly drama; and to transfer the conditions of Gerontius to an awareness in the world is surely in the interest of art and ultimately of argument, if that argument is to find vehicle in art. The danger of that procedure is that art will command ascendency over vision, at the expense of that seriousness of the feelings engaged by art, feelings which require a reconciliation of memory and desire more fully than aesthetics alone can manage. It is again the problem of the relation of being to form, of image to object and awareness. Or in a crude but practical reduction of the difficulty, of content to stanza. One might indeed hazard the conjecture after wrestling with the problem that "the care for perfection of form, among some of the romantic poets of the nineteenth century, was an effort. . . to conceal from view, an inner disorder."

The romantic critic such as Arnold, no less than the poet, has the problem to contend with. There is in Arnold, Eliot says in 1930, "a powerful element of Puritan morality," which when unyoked from Christianity runs into the future and empowers *Marius the Epicurean.* The New England intellectual dilemma of the relation of the Word to the world, from which Eliot flees by moving to England, reappears in strange places.

If it leads to the Gnosticism of pragmatism on this side of the Atlantic, it may lead to the Gnosticism of paganism in quiet, respectable Victorian minds like Arnold's, and Arnold's contribution to one's thought no less than Emerson's can blink the shadow of a Sweeney straddled in the sun. It does so when *Culture* is set in the place of *Religion,* through which manipulation, Eliot says, Arnold leaves "religion to be laid waste by the anarchy of feeling." Arnold's is an "intellectual epicureanism," through which occurs the "degradation of philosophy and religion." And Eliot adds, preparing to look into Pater, "Only when religion has been partly retired and confined, when an Arnold can sternly remind us that Culture is wider than Religion, do we get 'religious art' and in due course 'aesthetic religion.' " Arnold makes an interesting foil to Baudelaire in Eliot's thinking (though he does not yoke the two together beyond the serial appearance of the two essays in his *Selected Essays,* both of them written in 1930). We have seen Eliot arguing that Baudelaire's negativism is a descent into the terror of sin and degradation as a pursuit of some glimmer of beatitude, his poetry of flight being a willed encounter with evil. In contrast, Eliot finds Arnold's writings

> tediously negative. But they are negative in a peculiar fashion: their aim is to affirm that the emotions of Christianity can and must be preserved without the belief. From this proposition two different types of man can extract two different types of conclusion: (1) that Religion is Morals, (2) that Religion is Art. The effect of Arnold's religious campaign is to divorce Religion from thought.

On that competent continuation of degraded philosophy and religion, *Marius the Epicurean,* Eliot calls attention to Pater's tendency to "emphasize whatever is morbid or associated with physical malady." Pater himself points to the same inclination in Coleridge and in Pascal: the inexhaustible discontent, languor, and homesickness which, in Pater's phrase applied to Coleridge, echo an "endless regret." Pater is trying to escape such romanticism, into the religion of art for art's sake. He disguises, at least on the surface, that same element in himself which he rather unerringly fingers in Coleridge. He does so by the fiction of the romantic moment set in history. Pater narrates Marius's position on the threshold of the Church's establishment out of pagan Rome, with our own recent history (the years intervening between that ancient day and 1875) implied as if in the future of his suspended narration. But that trick of past history as prophecy of the future does not effectively answer the sense of disorder and endless regret to which Pater himself is subject. Art may be argued as coming to one, as Pater argues for it, "professing frankly to give nothing but the highest quality to your moments as they pass, and simply for their moment's sake." But it can do so only *innocently* by failing to recognize that it moves from philosophical and religious principles or *diabolically* in the interest of subversion. It does not satisfy desire by pretending that in memory, and through memory, we discover that every other moment of awareness, including Marius's in Rome, is like our own, "set between two hypothetical eternities" called the past and futre. Just how unsatisfactory that position is we find dramatized in the joyful agony of Pater's student, who fought himself clear of Pater's entrapment and on to a reconciliation of time past, present, and future. I refer to Gerard Manley Hopkins, who can come to an acceptance of the burnt-out ends of smoky days, move beyond them, and see the awesome beauty of decay as reflecting a permanence surer than the floating awareness which contains a thousand sordid images, constituting a soul, but an empty soul. In "Felix Randal," "Carrion Comfort," "The Windhover," "Pied Beauty," we have a mind convinced of its reconciliation of head and heart, so that we scarcely trouble ourselves to disengage in it the Romantic and the Classical. Hopkins has arrived at a position we see Eliot painfully struggling toward in *The Waste Land* and he too arrives after a journey not unlike Baudelaire's. Eliot's arrival is just ahead of us.

XIII

THE TURNING FROM TIRESIAS

in the brown baked features
The eyes of a familiar compound ghost
Both intimate and unidentifiable.
So I assumed a double part, and cried
And heard another's cry: 'What! are *you* here?'
Although we were not.

Little Gidding

That disembodied, floating consciousness of the first part of *The Waste Land*, to which Eliot attaches the name Tiresias, is dawning to the deceptiveness of reason and the senses, and more importantly to the impossibility of their being reconciled unaided. As Pascal observed of them, these "two principles of truth [reason and the senses] are not only both not genuine, but are engaged in mutual deception." In the throes of the human condition, whose marks Pascal identifies as "inconstancy, boredom, anxiety," only the heart may find the way beyond the deception. He does not mean heart in the sentimental usage the word acquires in the decay of language during this and the last century, a decay which leaves *heart* stranded along with *angel* and *soul* in the lyrics of popular songs and sentimental poetry. Pascal means it rather as Dante does, and as the medievalist means it. It is the heart which is the seat of charity and the fountain of intuitive knowledge, a knowledge sounder than the easy acceptance of "feelings" as the engine to lay waste religion, as Eliot has it in his criticism of Arnold. That Arnoldian havoc is also at the expense of reason, being in part a revolt against that dominance of reason—at least at the theoretical level—in the eighteenth century. It is well to remember that just before Eliot wrote *The Waste Land* he had been reading intensively in nineteenth century literature for courses he was teaching for the money necessary to make ends meet. When we add to that necessity his own affinities to nineteenth century romanticism but his lack of ease with some of the English writers of the period, we discover that the burden of his objections to them centers around what he considered their intellectual carelessness. He will charge Arnold with a looseness of terms, but he has already attacked a carelessness in Wordsworth's unrefined use of *emotion* in relation to *feeling*.

For Eliot, the unexamined term is not worth using. *Emotion* or *feeling* may have betrayal implicit in them for the unwary. The careless mind may mistake wishful thinking for vision or insight, and mistake an emotional response as a spiritual growth of the mind. The image may be clothed with one's feeling, suspended in consciousness, so that awareness may mistake its own existence as the life of the "out there." However, Eliot even though a student of philosophy cannot finally grant preeminence to reason, for reason unaided cannot break through that closed world of the self which reason itself has established. What the self knows most absolutely is its own entrapment, which it considers against the postulate of an "out there," some "other," or (sub genera) *past, present, future.* Confident at best only of its own existence—its own "inconstancy, boredom, anxiety"—it is denied its inexplicable hunger for infinitude by the memory, which forces upon its consideration the demon of time-space. Still, in the midst of the sordid and empty which *The Waste Land* suspends, whatever its causes there is yet that unnamed desire, which neither happy nor unhappy relations with the world of objects alone will satisfy. It is the desire for that condition of being Wordsworth declared himself to have experienced, though infrequently, those "spots of time." That condition Eliot will subsequently identify as the still point of the turning world, once he has come to see the world as not so narrowly circumscribed as in the "Preludes." But words will have to be emptied and filled again before he can name that condition of simplicity in which he has learned to care and not to care.

As Eliot recognized in his discomfort with the intellectual carelessness in the nineteenth century mind, a problem with the mystical approach to existence lies with names. The feeling one has (but from whence he can hardly say since he is left looking into the heart of silence in a stillness which does not answer) is that if the name could be spoken the veils of the self would be rent. That feeling leads to incantation, a dominant concern in nineteenth century poetry such as one finds it in Shelley's "Ode to the West Wind" or Whitman's "Out of the Cradle Endlessly Rocking." But it is too easy an out to accept as mystical experience an emotional and intellectual bafflement expressed in a more or less rhythmical way. To the extent that incantation through words fails, the temptation to other devices used for the same end flourishes. The recourse to drugs seems often to be out of the failure in one's using words as prayer wheels in the river of rhythm. But mysticism requires an address of the mind to mystery in a severely disciplined way, in which address reason itself has an important role. Because Dante must turn from Virgil at the summit of Mt. Purgatory does not mean that he had no need of Virgil in getting that far. One begins to enter a plane higher than reason can bring him to when he realizes that the inadequacy of names lies in their being incommensurate to the essence they are necessary instruments toward. One must, through reason, come to terms with the limits of the discursive mind as it is defined by Plato and Aristotle and baptized by Augustine and Aquinas. The movement along this path in Eliot, during which names—words—are emptied and so transcended or refilled, is very marked in his poetry: we notice an acceptance of failure and inadequacy in "Gerontion," in which rocks, moss, stonecrop, iron, merds, Mr. Silvero, Hakagawa are accepted as empty shuttles weaving the wind in an empty head. We come at last to *give, sympathize, control,* only less empty than Gerontion's words because of a moment's surrender of the self; we come to the laborious and tortuous ascent of the stairs of self-forgetfulness in "Ash-Wednesday," in which at last we find reconciled the disparity between Christ's passion for the world which the Christian would emulate and man's passion for the worldly which threatens him. The region of "Ash-Wednesday," as we have said, is the shores of Lethe on Dante's mountain, where at last the puzzle of the Word within the word, Christ the tiger, becomes a reassuring paradox through which one at last sees beauty pied, with a memory transformed:

> See, now they vanish,
> The faces and the places, with the self which,
>   as it could, loved them,
> To become renewed,—transfigured, in another pattern.

Eliot's intellectual and spiritual direction works against the possibilities of dramatic poetry, though the impassioned lyric of a Hopkins is not precluded, and though Eliot himself wins through to remarkably effective verse plays. His direction works against drama as certainty always works against poetry, evidence of which we have seen in Newman's attempt to cast his certainty in art. For art becomes dead when discovery both precedes it and ceases to accompany it. Eliot makes much of the importance of doubt to Pascal, because doubt alone can make the wager dramatic. So long as doubt is at least an element in the poet's journey, Satan can be persuasive in one's *Paradise Lost,* though the more conjured doubt itself becomes, the less persuasive. Put another way, the absence of doubt in the soul alive is the deepest of silences. And though the most desirable of human conditions, that absence makes art unnecessary. One

never hears of Adam or Eve singing in Eden. That is the point
Jacques Maritain is making in *Creative Intuition in Art and
Poetry* (1952) when he says, "Poetic experience is from the start
oriented toward expression and terminated in a word uttered or
a work produced; while mystical experience tends toward silence,
and terminates in an immanent fruition of the Absolute." In this
light, Eliot's plays become, like Milton's *Paradise Regained,*
the compromise he makes with silence.

A revealing analogue to "Ash-Wednesday" and one which
parallels the movement I am describing in Eliot's poetry in
general is in Chapter 10, Book 9 of Augustine's *Confessions.* It
is his "Vision at Ostia," which occurred after the burning journey
to Rome echoed by Eliot in the closing lines of "The Fire Sermon." There Augustine recounts an experience of this movement toward silence, beyond language. After the literal journey,
he and St. Monica rest in a house on the Tiber. They stand looking out into its garden from an elevation, putting the past behind
them and so reaching finally beyond the future. In their talk
of the moment he says, "We proceeded step by step through
all bodily things up to that heaven whence shine the sun and the
moon. . . We ascended higher yet by means of inward thought
and discourse and admiration of your [God's] works, and we
came up to our own minds. We transcended them." Of the state
of vision achieved: "to have been and to be in the future do not
belong to it, but only to be. . .we turned back again to the noise
of our mouths, where a word both begins and ends." In that
moment of beatitude, a man has passed "beyond himself by not
thinking upon himself." And in that state of silence beyond
words he hears creation speak out clearly: "We did not make
ourselves, but he who endures forever made us." In the ascent
to a higher *silence*—and *silence* is a word which enters Eliot's
poetry insistently in *The Waste Land*—one goes beyond the
created world, which includes oneself and his words, and arrives
at (as Augustine puts it) "his Word not uttered by tongues of
flesh, nor by angel's voice, 'nor by the sound of thunder,' nor by
the riddle of similitude." Augustine's vision returns to time and
self, to the point from which the elevation of the soul began in
words, and when he has returned he sees the place with eyes very
like those reentering the garden at the end of *Little Gidding.*

What we notice particularly to our purpose in Augustine's
words here is that they so aptly characterize the struggle larger

than the poetic which *The Waste Land* signifies. The struggle
with the "riddle of similitude" is everywhere present, as in the
last section of the poem which is concerned with "What the
Thunder Said." In 1933 Eliot attempts to describe a kind of
poetry which has moved beyond signification, through incantation, and into a condition of transparency. Eliot finds himself in
accord with D. H. Lawrence's call for a poetry of "stark, bare,
rocky directness of statement":

> This speaks to me of that at which I have long aimed, in
> writing poetry; to write poetry which should be essen-
> tially poetry, with nothing poetic about it, poetry stand-
> ing naked in its bare bones, or poetry so transparent that
> we should not see the poetry, but that which we are
> meant to see through the poetry. . . To get *beyond*
> poetry. . .

(The passage is quoted from an unpublished lecture by Eliot
"English Letter Writers" delivered at New Haven, Connecticut,
quoted by F. O. Matthiessen in *The Achievement of T. S. Eliot*.)
Eliot develops the position further in "The Music of Poetry"
(1942) as he is finishing the last of the *Quartets*.

Because Eliot cannot name that condition which will allow
him to get beyond poetry and because the body of his work
constitutes a search for that name, one concludes *The Waste
Land* incomplete, though its incompleteness does not mean
it lacks unity. It represents a considerable moment in that
sequence of "naming" moments from the "Preludes" to *Little
Gidding*. We encounter the journey on the surface of his poetry,
but it is the dramatic moment rather than the narrative sequence
which is important. The narrative elements are but correlatives
for a movement of the mind. To see this distinction is to reconcile the fragmentary appearance of the poem to our aesthetic
demands for unity in the poem. The burden of Eliot's drama,
private and public, is the riddle of fragmentation itself, which
the poet attempts to solve with Augustine's "riddle of similitude." To that fragmentation, the reason can give only a semblance of order. One sees the struggle toward ordered rest in
relation to the world immediately adjacent to the senses, the expression of which relationship is necessarily sequential and therefore in the direction of narrative. In "The Fire Sermon" we
notice that the place names plot a course from West London

along the Thames and down to the coast at Margate Sands. Also interwoven with the immediate geography is the journey of memory—history by allusion from Elizabethan England to the 1920s. The poem as a whole contains a history of English poetry through its borrowings and imitations—from Chaucer's April version of the Thames, which historically opens out upon the larger world of English nationalism, echoed by Eliot from Spenser's view of the Thames. There is the presence also of Pope's more caustic evaluation of that spirit, which expires upon the banks of the turgid river in 1922, where rats drag bellies and all the "nymphs" are departed out of foul weather.

There is, then, a pattern to Eliot's appropriations, though not a pattern requiring the orderlines Joyce brings to his parody of the history of English prose in *Ulysses.* We recall once more Eliot's welcome of *Ulysses* in his review of it published the year after *The Waste Land:* "Instead of the narrative method, we may now use the mythical method." A hopeful and enthusiastic note, but not spoken with a full understanding of the implication of his search for the key to selection or exclusion of images and ideas. For the burden of mind itself is discursiveness, and the history of the mind is its narrative journey, occasionally arrested, in moments of release, in a spot of time or at some still point. Art may come close to escaping that sequential enslavement of the mind which makes one long for the state of Milton's angels, but even there, and even in the most abstract painting, the mind must be brought into the gallery, into the presence of the work, and if one notice carefully, all else still, the eye moves if ever so slightly. Not even Sophocles can escape the "narrative" trap, since *Oedipus Rex* itself constitutes a series of moments, separate frames of a magic lantern that casts a movement toward a full knowledge.

Eliot's pattern of selection and exclusion requires an inclusive representation. To imitate the action of a disordered and confused awareness through a perfection of form such as the nineteenth century poet might bring to the problem would be to conceal the underlying disorder. To discover a principle of exclusion, a control of disorder beyond the simplicity of sequence— "the narrative method"—is possible to Pound, the outsider, as it was not at the moment to Eliot. Pound can look at the manuscript and declare that the poem begins with the cruelty of April and ends with *shantih.* Eliot's personal experience in a Boston bar or of New England sailing is material not necessary to the deeper personal experience of the conversion of a mind. Neither is the direct attempt to imitate Pope, nor the attempt to out-Browning Browning in "The Death of the Duchess." But the real burden of Eliot's poem, Pound was in no state of mind to appreciate. The quest for that key to unlock the self from its closed, fragmentary state was not to issue upon action such as Pound could envisage, having himself recently shaken the dust of decayed London from his heels; the turning of that key left Eliot seemingly passive, where the poet to Pound was required by the age to be activist.

Of course, we may believe Eliot when he says of his his experience with *The Waste Land,* "To me it was only the relief of a personal and wholly insignificant grouse against life; it is just a piece of rhythmical grumbling." But one does not measure the spiritual significance and magnitude of the soul's turning openly to the world in terms of its spectacle. That one could bring himself to attempt to give, sympathize and control at the level below that of spectacle suggests that he is ceasing to be childish. Why don't you control your temper, and sympathize with Bobby and give him your toy train for a little while? Significant moments in one's spiritual development seen in retrospect often appear sophomoric, but Eliot's *only* and *just,* which reduce the experience to an adolescent level, are not sufficient to the magnitude of his experience.

The key we keep talking about is not *give, sympathize, control,* though those words are the ones we usually concentrate most heavily upon in our reading of *The Waste Land.* We can hardly escape that temptation, Eliot having highlighted them for us with his *Datta, Dayadhvam, Damyata.* And his footnote pointing us to the Upanishads has moved us a world away in time, space, and climate of thought. What those elements in the poem suggest is the first movements out of the closed self into a new disorder and fragmentation. But the new disorder is discovered with changed eyes; the silence into which it looks is beginning to speak back, and out of the fragments that are spoken the new consciousness can at last begin to set its own house in order.

It is at this point that Eliot breaks rather sharply with Pound, though it is a break more easily seen in retrospect than

Pound could notice at the time, or Eliot himself for that matter. Pound can wisely argue for the exclusion of the line from St. John which Eliot was tempted to insert in the first draft of "The Burial of the Dead," ("I John saw these things, and heard them"). They do violate most noticeably the point of view that Eliot associates with the name Tiresias. But the awareness is not so easily characterized by that name in the final section. Of course, Pound could heartily approve of the intention the awareness expresses: to set its own house in order. It is the sermon he preaches most resolutely in Canto XIII, with the aid of Confucius. In that Canto, we are exhorted to practice brotherly deference, to see in what ways we are members one of another. Confucius emphasizes Pound's argument that without order in one's own mind there can be no order in the man, nor in his family, nor the state—a sequence of Chinese boxes whose most important one is the outer one, the state. But Pound makes emphatic an old point of his:

> Kung gave the words "order"
> and "brotherly deference"
> And said nothing of the "life after death."

Pound's position in that Canto bears remarkable correspondence to St. Paul's argument for our contentment "each in his nature," that is, each within the limits of his talent.

> For as we have many members in one body, and all members have not the same office: So we, being many, are one body in Christ, and every one members one of another; Having then gifts differing according to the grace that is given us. . . Be kindly affectionate one to another with brotherly love.

Thus in Pound's Canto Tian will take up charioteering; Tseu-lou put the defenses in order; Khieu be lord of a province; Tchi devote himself to the priesthood of the mind; and Tian, the low speaking, devote himself to the music of words. And each has chosen the highest calling, because each chooses within the limits of his gift. As to whether a man should hide and protect his son who has committed murder, Kung says only that "He should hide him." It is the question St. Augustine contends with in a commentary on the Psalms in which David protests false appearances, the deceitfulness in man which constitutes lying.

Augustine says

> . . .it is one thing to tell a lie, another to pass the truth
> over in silence. If. . .we would avoid exposing a man to
> the risk of death, we must be prepared to conceal the
> truth but not to tell an untruth. We must either expose
> him or lie, otherwise we shall kill our own soul for the
> sake of another man's body.

Similarities between Pound's and Confucius's message and
St. Paul's and Augustine's are rather obvious. But what is decisive—and what shows most clearly the separation of ways between Pound and Eliot—is the contrast in the ends. In Pound,
there is a concern for the whole state of the state; in Paul and
Augustine a concern for the whole state of the individual soul.
In Paul, the members one of another constitute a body "in
Christ." To lie, as Augustine says, is to deny the individual soul
its rest in Christ. In Pound one hides his son, but does not protect him; to protect him would constitute revolt against the state.
In a position which can say nothing of "the life after death," the
state must be supreme, since the concept of order must exhibit
itself in time. It is Pound's version of the Puritan ethic which he
so vehemently attacked. What he does is substitute: where
worldly accomplishment, as in the acquisition of the world's
goods through the ordering of nature, reflects a progress toward
the transcendent world (an aspect of Puritanism that troubles
Hawthorne in "Young Goodman Brown"), individual order, reflected in the ordered community, marks a progress toward the
ideal state, Ecbatan or the city of Dioce.

Eliot's words out of Isaiah, "Shall I at least set my lands in
order," may appear to Pound in accord with his own position;
but it is no more so than are Paul's and Augustine's compatible
to Confucius's and Pound's. In the beginning, as Eliot says in
"Tradition and the Individual Talent," he has been "struggling
to attack" a point of view which is "perhaps related to the metaphysical theory of the substantial unity of the soul." His *substantial* is the operative word; Eliot is a philosopher and he uses
the technical word deliberately. But through the personal experience of which *The Waste Land* is historical evidence, he has
come to abandon that struggle. Feelings, emotions, reason,
thought, awareness itself must have a more inclusive embodi-
ment. From this point on, he will be affirming the substantial

unity of the soul, a unity victim to the perversity of its own will, whose only corrective lies in one's spitting out the seeds of the wrath-bearing tree. His affirmation requires, as he sees, not a repudiation of the necessity of "brotherly deference," nor of the state, but rather a larger Chinese box than Pound will allow, in which to include the individual member and the state. He is becoming concerned with the idea of a Christian society as a consequence of a new belief in the substantial unity of the individual soul.

Pound's position affords no explanation of perversity except as error; though he deals with ignorance in a tone suggesting he takes it as malignant, his principles will not allow it to be argued as such. It does not mean that he can write no persuasvie poetry; indeed one might argue such a disparity as the very cause of some of his greatest poetry. We have only to compare the didactic concern with "brotherly deference" in Canto XIII to the moving circumstance of his mind caught up by memory in the cage at Pisa, where (if anywhere along the way) Pound acts out Paul's exhortation that we be kindly affectionate one to another. The *Pisan Cantos* are, in this respect, Pound's *Waste Land*. There is in Eliot's consent to set his own lands in order the tone and implication of that quieter statement of the point we have already noted. In *The Rock* he will assert the desert not "remote" or "around the corner" but in one's own "heart." Therefore, *"Make perfect your will."* In doing so, one escapes Prufrock's dilemma of the opposition of knowing and action, between which falls the deadly shadow. One can both act and know the limitations of his action, but one does not thereby "neglect or belittle the desert." Thus Eliot can conclude that Pound's version of the mind in nature—in the desert—has no way of accounting for the individual, and hence no way of explaining individual talent except ultimately as an accident of nature. In turning from such a question, Pound allows the unexamined individual will to be elevated in his thought to the supreme position, however fortunately it may be endowed with a capacity for brotherly deference, as Pound's was. The larger Chinese box which Pound refuses when he insists that Kung says nothing of the life after death is the very one which Dante celebrates, leading him to rest authority in the Church over the state, in spite of the corruptions he excoriates, and it is to Augustine through Dante, rather than Confucius through Pound, that Eliot takes his way. Thus, to see oneself in relation to the Lighted City of

Augustine, beyond Baudelaire's *fourmillante cité*, is to be able to declare without hopelessness or despair that

> if blood of Martyrs is to flow on the steps
> We must first build the steps,
> And if the Temple is to be cast down
> We must first build the Temple.

XIV

AND PAST ILLEGIBLE STONES

Every phrase and every sentence is an end and a beginning,
Every poem an epitaph.

Little Gidding

Gerhart Neimeyer, in his *Between Paradise and Nothingness,* comments on a social order based on a public past in contrast to one based on cosmological myth. He is adapting, in his comparison of Israel to Egypt and Mesopotamia, the evidence and arguments of Eric Voegelin to his concern for the development of modern political and social institutions, and his address to that subject makes his work and Voegelin's of particular interest to Eliot's concern for myth. The rediscovery of myth's ordering potential, Eliot said in his discussion of *Ulysses,* provides "a method for which the horoscope is auspicious." Eliot's wit in the comment is not overwhelming, nor was the discovery so propitious as it seemed, Eliot becoming in a sense the victim of myth rather than its manipulator for the sake of art. As Neimeyer remarks, "In the order of the myth, the past was not differentiated from the present and neither was the future." Eliot, in announcing myth's rescue of modern art, is doing so at a point where history's issue is a fragmented civilization in which memory allows only nightmare as an answer to desire, desire at best appearing to be merely wishful thinking when pursued desperately in the memory.

And, while Eliot's specific myth is at that moment anchored in Greece and Rome, new myths are beginning to evolve around him to devour the very conception of human existence Eliot wants to rescue. The flourishing of Freudian psychology and Marxian conception of history spring resolutely out of determinist thinking developed out of the Renaissance, about which Eliot is already having second thoughts, as the allusions of *The Waste Land* suggest. For the varying shades of determinism were ruthlessly appropriating all history to the cause and associating a "narrative method" with emerging myths, positing worldly goals to be realized through myth—social or economic adjustment to result in Utopian ends. Eliot's projection of art's horoscope under the influence of myth proved premature. The differentiation of time past and time future in relation to time present in the new myths, with which differentiation he will wrestle in *Burnt Norton,* commanded hope in the confused Western mind, and hence made possible power to the new myths. That power radically undermined the conception of man's place in the universe as lying within an omniscient and omnipotent power of a first cause, which Eliot was to come to rest in finally. But he was already in some degree aware of the difficulty not only in the new myths, but in the old ones out of pagan worlds. He is reserved in his use of Jessie Weston's ideas on ritual and romance, anchored as those ideas are not in revelation—that intrusion into time whereby a closed cosmological system such as the Egyptian and Mesopotamian and Greek and Roman is ruptured—but in repetition and re-enactment which negate transcendence, leaving man's end an endless circling within a cosmological cage. It has become increasingly apparent that the modern myths of man's destiny, established on the unsupportable differentiations of time past, present, and future such as Neimeyer examines critically, practiced an illusion of progress to hold captive the sources of power through hope while obscuring the reality of the new myths' cosmological cage. The illusive problem of psychological norms, the repeated projection of five-year plans have required an elaborate rhetoric that resulted in such a decay of language that Eliot recognizes at last the poet's primary responsiblity as the purifying of that language.

Cosmological symbolism such as that of the Egyptians, Neimeyer suggests, is informed and formed by myth. "In so far as men structure their common life with a view to nature hierophanies of various sorts, they do so by reenacting the myth of creation, destruction and regeneration, being and coming-to-be, and the unity of all life in its multiple forms." Such an approach to the problem of being gives rise to a body of vigorous poetry such as that upon which Eric Voegelin bases much of his study in the first volumes of *Order and History*. Poetry from Homer at least through Virgil—since it is that line of the poets which most directly affects the Western tradition—shares heavily a closed cosmological system, though that very system contributes to a sense of organic unity such as is aesthetically useful to poetry. One finds in Eliot's favorite, Aeschylus, such questioning as attempts to break out of the closed system, as in those heretical questions voiced by the chorus of the *Agamemnon* about the names of the Gods or God as man's attempt to name the ineffable transcendent. Aeschylus' is an attempt through intellect to break out of the enclosing myth, as opposed to that experience of the Israelites in the desert that Voegelin concentrates upon in *Israel and Revelation.* As Neimeyer says, "The refugees of the Sea of Reeds experienced God in the single event of their deliverance." They are never the same people again, nor is Western history ever the same, an awareness of which historical fact intrudes upon Eliot's mind as he is writing "By the waters of Leman I sat down and wept." in "The Fire Sermon." That thought is completed in Psalm 137: "How shall we sing the Lord's song in a strange land?" The effect of that intrusion of revelation upon Western awareness is an explosion of the closed cosmological system for Israel, prelude to a second explosion in Voegelin's estimate, the discovery of philosophy by the Greek mind.

But the second effective blow to the lingering cosmological entrapment of the West, at least from Eliot's point of view revealed as it emerges in *The Waste Land,* is the Advent. In the world that follows, the poet's old concern for the complexity of time and place is made even more complex in its attempt to deal with the mystery of being. Our own world's inclination to restore closed system, given impetus by eighteenth century philosophy and nineteenth century science, had proved all but universally successful by World War II. It was a system so closed as to make of all existence an uncaused mechanism, man included, and the emerging new myths we have spoken of—principally Darwinism, Freudianism, and Marxism—worked hand in glove to accomplish that enclosure. For Freudianism reads the individual existence as a closed cosmological system, its mechanism internal, so that the self is a sort of atom of random power. Marxian thought builds upon an aggregate of such atoms, evolving a force in history whose conception of the social lacks a sense of organic community in which might be recognized any viable hierarchy of being. Life itself is radically redefined; and, in so far as the new conception of existence lends itself to poetry, the source of metaphorical terms lies in mechanics or chemistry, and in that substitute for Platonic Idea, abstract mathematics, which operates at the local level (if the local may even be said to exist) as statistics. *Fact* is the person of *number,* as it were. (Jung's divergence from Freud is, in this light, reactionary, returning to organic community in such a way as to at least enlarge the cosmological entrapment beyond mechanism.)

The ancient cosmology which Voegelin examines was at least a self-contained organism, and as such amenable to celebra-

tion by the sympathetic poet. In the nineteenth century, it becomes the poet's elected task to resist mechanical doctrine. One
may see the attempt in Coleridge's theory of poetry as organic,
the single most influential idea out of the nineteenth century
upon the poetry of the twentieth. One sees the same resistance
in Walt Whitman's attempt to rescue the organic, not by argument, but by the act of his poetry, though Whitman's "self" is
different in an important respect from Coleridge's. Imagination,
in the famous definition of the *Biographia Literaria,* is anchored
in its Primary dimension in the Great I AM, while Whitman is
more closely allied in his inclination to those more ancient poets
who celebrate the self as the cosmological world. That Eliot is
aware of such a distinction and both pays Whitman his respect
and parts company with him is suggested in his echoes of Whitman's thrush in *The Waste Land.* The hermit-thrush singing in
the pine trees, to which Eliot gives us reference in Chapman's
Handbook of Birds of Eastern North America, has its source
of reference more directly in Whitman's "wondrous chant of
the gray-brown bird" of "When Lilacs Last in the Dooryard
Bloomed." The allusion to that experience on the road to
Emmaus in Luke, needs comparing as well to Whitman's "panorama of visions" in sections 15 and 16 of that poem to see the
sharpness of Eliot's turning away from Whitman's version of a
closed world of the self. (We might note in passing that Eliot's
younger contemporary, Hart Crane, makes heroic attempt to
reconcile the organic and mechanistic being in *The Bridge,*
through the mind as medium, being a cosmological poet like
Whitman, rather than a poet like Coleridge or Eliot after *The
Waste Land.*)

By the time of *The Bridge,* which is in part a reaction to
Eliot, Eliot himself is finding a new way that requires a different
address to myth. It is not a mechanism within the inventive
powers of the poet, nor may it be imported out of history to
the rescue of form by an act of the intellect. The "mythical
method" appears increasingly a sign of an intrinsic reality of
creation long neglected, and in its invocation by man a spiritual
necessity, not an intellectual invention. In short, where Eliot
had thought it possible to use myth, he was discovering himself
used by myth. At the same time, the "Classical" attempt he has
pursued is beginning to appear a pagan attempt to Eliot in his
reading of his own dilemma. Dante has proved for him a truer
father of the spirit than the cosmologically confined poets, even

a poet like Virgil, though that very change in Eliot's understanding in one sense makes his appreciation of the Classical poets deeper. For that change makes him more perceptive of those poets' struggle with inadequacy, the struggle which leads Dante to glorify the five great pagan poets, while at the same time confining them to Limbo.

Thus Eliot perceives that Tiresias must either die or be baptized if his own world is to be reconciled to a transcendent cause. To surrender to that cause, however, requires of Eliot a sacrifice more difficult than it would seem to a mind possessed either by scientific determinism or liberated in the cosmological ecstasy of the self.

In considering Eliot's position as it may be reflected in his poetry, one must remember that distinction to be made between our imposition of a narrative structure upon his development, which the very discussion of the problem threatens to impose by its discursive necessity, and the reality of that development in Eliot himself, a reality which we can never enter fully into, though we need not be so bleakly convinced of an absolute separation of his world from our own as his Bradley footnote suggests. Eliot, for instance, is drawn to a Virgil or a Whitman by a part of his nature which is not destroyed by his changed view of man's place in nature. There was from the beginning also, as a part of his personality, an element of the sophisticated aesthete, the man of the modern world which so puzzled Bertrand Russell in the Harvard seminar. Eliot's casual yoking of Heraclitus and Villon has about it a gesture out of ennui such as settled upon the young intellectual of artistic bent in the wake of the *Yellow Book* and the Rhymers Club and all the progeny of Pater. One finds traces of that spirit in Pound and Joyce and Hume, and on and on. So that partly from a literary inheritance and partly from personal bent, that influence continues awhile in Eliot, to be discovered I think in his prose style. It is reflected also in his rather superficial disdain of nineteenth century poets, particularly of Wordsworth and Tennyson, which he will later regret and attempt to rectify, the sort of disdain which seems inevitable in one who sees himself in his fathers but has not yet recognized the likeness. (The outsider is often more acutely aware of family resemblance than the member of the family.)

In this complex of spiritual and intellectual being are the

elements which prepare the ground for an engaging poetry, that poetry of the struggle of the self caught in a dilemma in which the self seems required to surrender to chaos, since reason can make no pattern to justify desire. But that sturggle is not separated out into constituent ideas and elements in a sequence of poems. The very pattern of Eliot's poetry is nevertheless a constant vision and revision of fragments saved out of the continuing struggle. "That's one way in which my mind does seem to have worked throughout the years poetically—doing things separately and then seeing the possibility of fusing them together, altering them, and making a kind of whole of them." Thus Eliot in the *Paris Review* interview late in life. But it is not simply the poetical operation of his mind. It is most particularly a spiritual mode, in which Eliot revisits and redigests past experience, lest having had the experience he may have missed the meaning. Eliot could no more engage himself in a process such as commits Pound to the *Cantos* than he could set a series of experiences as a regime out of which to condense poetry. There is, one might say, a stumbling tediousness about Eliot, as compared to such a flamboyant mind as Pound's, but it does not reflect simply an analytical accumulation of the materials of memory. He relives the past experience from an enlarged perspective upon it, in which he most resembles Wordsworth. Poetry is emotion re-collected in whatever tranquility the growth of being allows in the interval from the original experience.

     In Rilke there is a statement which may help clarify the point I am struggling to make:

> In order to write a single verse, one must see many cities and men and things; one must get to know animals and the flight of birds, and the gestures that the little flowers make when they open out in the morning. . . There must be memories of many nights of love, each one unlike the others. . . One must also have been beside the dying, must have sat beside the dead. And still it is not yet enough to have memories. . . Only when they have been turned to blood within us. . .only then can it happen that in a most rare hour the first word of a poem arises in their midst and goes forth from them.

Thus speaks another of the cosmological poets of such a range of experience as Eliot's Tiresias recalls, who has sat below the walls of Thebes and walked among the lowest of the dead. But it is the suggestion that memories must be turned to blood within us for the sake of poetry that I call attention to. Poetry is the flower of blooded memory, one might say. And the meaning of the word of a poem as it first rises in the midst of such memory, to the poet, is not fully available, as Eliot will emphasize in the *Quartets*, those explications by Eliot of the meaning in the earlier poetry. In addition, that blooding of memory is never at an end until the end. Every moment is a crucial encounter, in which the multiple and conflicting pulls of being are in a tension whose issue is in doubt. Eliot survives his poetry to say at last that it is through grace, through the voice of that Calling which is Love, that the closed self and its conflicting wills is opened, but opened without the self's being thereby exploded into nothingness by the cataclysm—that danger that threatens a Poe or Rimbaud, Verlaine, Mallarmé.

The reflective poet's circumstance in the midst of his making is quite different from the circumstance of the critic who approaches a body of poetry signified as *Complete*. It would take, I suspect, a sensibility such as that of Pascal or Kierkegaard to realize a continuing agitation in *The Four Quartets*, a work which strikes the more casual reader as a falling off after the desperate intensity of *The Waste Land,* the price of which intensity is the appearance of fragmentation. I wish to suggest that there is an intensity in the *Quartets*, beneath the more carefully controlled form, of a degree we do not always acknowledge. It is as if the fact that Eliot needed no Pound to help him shape those poems makes us see them as the calm resolution of what was to Eliot surely a continuing struggle, in which each moment is one of decisive risk. On the other hand, I wish to suggest as well that *The Waste Land* has a dramatic movement, an effective one in spite of or even because of its being obscured by the fragmentary surface. The poem reaches its turning point in the silence between lines 7 and 8 of "Death by Water," a moment of surrender which has an effect analogous to Oedipus' cry of WOE at the climax of his journey of knowledge. The difference is that Oedipus' cry is one from which there is no sufficient recovery. Sophocles' world is still the closed world, however much there is flirtation with the transcendent in him. Socrates will question that closed world most effectively, with the immediate personal consequences that allowed Plato a dramatic center about which to order that questioning, Socrates' execution in 399.

Eliot's turning from the modern pagan world brought no such spectacular nemesis, though it did spark the occasional sarcasm of Pound and led, we are told, to a strained moment with Eliot's old teacher, Irving Babbitt, in the late 1920's. Earlier in that decade, young Leo Strauss, observing the resurgence of theology all about him on the continent, asked his teacher Edmund Husserl about the strange development. Husserl responded, "If there is a datum 'God' we shall describe it." Eliot was at that moment abandoning that last hope of rescue from the closed cosmological world of the self promised by phenomenology. His note quoting Bradley and attached to *The Waste Land*'s turning key, indicates the abandonment. Strauss concludes about that turning, which was happening all about him, that the spiritual resurgence in the modern world "was in fact a profound innovation," though scoffed at by Husserl. There was the beginning of a new possibility for Christian society. When Eliot comes to discuss that possibility in old age, some twenty years later, he will pose the term pagan to supersede his more usual term Classical. And looking back upon his long engagement of that term, he will say, near the end of his life, "as for Classicism and Romanticism, I find the terms have no longer the importance to me that they once had." They could not to one who had come to see the terms applied to different addresses to the world, neither of which solved the larger problem of the spiritual quest and its resolution. Both terms addressed the same world, that world which a despairing school of writers was to declare after World War II to have no exit. The exit for Eliot lay through the waste land of the self, an intolerable country until its chaos was surrendered in response to that Calling which made it possible at last for him to accept and live with the realization that

> Every phrase and every sentence is an end and a beginning,
> Every poem an epitaph. And any action
> Is a step to the block, to the fire, down the sea's throat
> Or to an illegible stone: and that is where we start.

XV

THE AWFUL DARING

So I assumed a double part, and cried
And heard another's voice cry: 'What! are *you* here?'
Although we were not. I was still the same,
  Knowing myself yet being someone other—
  And he a face still forming.

Little Gidding

Though *The Waste Land* is the drama of a quest for a key, the necessity of which Eliot is painfully and personally aware of, one need not expect to find that key named this early in the quest. Not that there isn't a word for that key in 1922. But it rather appears that Eliot senses it necessary to act toward that word for the sake of dramatic tensions in his poetry. Yet more than poetry is at stake; perhaps the deferred naming is necessary as well to the rescue of the poet himself. The word becomes, for the mind struggling toward it, an objective correlative to be earned. In so far as Eliot is unable to escape this shadow upon vision, his thinking is still colored by its Puritan origins. There remains a clouding, a lingering suggestion that grace is to be earned by a fearful industry. If this be the state of mind in which *The Waste Land* is written, we may value more the torment of hope in "Ash-Wednesday" as the voice pleads, "Teach us to care and not to care/Teach us to sit still." For the most difficult of all hurdles to get beyond in the spiritual journey Eliot is set upon is that one requiring the acceptance of an incommensurate gift. One opens to an unearned Correlative that unifies more than one's sensibilities at the still point of the turning world, though it cost (or seems to cost) one nothing less than everything. We catch a glimpse of a joyful release Eliot was beginning to experience in the 1930's when he speaks in *Burnt Norton* of

> The inner freedom from the practical desire,
> The release from action and suffering, release from the
>   inner
> And the outer compulsion, yet surrounded
> By a grace of senses. . . .

For our understanding of an emotional force in such lines, we must read them against that earlier poetry.

If *The Waste Land* is a spectacle of the empty and sordid and bored world, if after the journey of memory which is made to parallel Eliot's literal journey out of London to Margate Sands the poem's voice can still connect nothing with nothing, the very desire to overcome the agony implies possibility. Absence and vacuum imply even a logical necessity of presence and object, give hope of the missing word no less than of the missing condition of being that may yet be recovered. That missing word hovers about the poem, in both the public and private versions of it: an unsaid and terrifying and hence perpetually disturbing word. The point is worth emphasizing, since Eliot has difficulty bringing himself to utter the word, a hesitant state he will look back upon in the opening lines of the fifth section of "Ash-Wednesday":

> If the lost word is lost, if the spent word is spent
> If the unheard, unspoken
> Word is unspoken, unheard;
> Still is the unspoken word, the Word unheard,
> The Word without a word, the Word within
> The world and for the world;
> And the light shone in darkness and
> Against the Word the unstilled world still whirled
> About the center of the silent Word.

These lines recall and imitate the earlier *Waste Land* panic through rhetorical incantation of emptied words. There is no imagery one can comfortably rest the lines in, yet they are not abstract. The play of time and movement, rest and the timeless, in such words as *still, silent, light* are *Waste Land* images emptied of the old inadequate particularity of their use in that earlier poem. And the quotation "O my people, what have I done unto thee," out of Micah, relates a point in the history of the race to Eliot's own history: a point just before the dawning of that Light. The Word, the perfect Stillness, Eliot comes to see as waiting the deliberate acceptance (or rejection) of the pilgrim in the desert of the world.

Eliot hovers in the shadows of *The Waste Land*'s irony, but he is less protected there than he has been in "Prufrock" or "Mr. Eliot's Sunday Morning."   For he is much nearer a new threshold, though unable to move across into a new country that bekons. It is the country of paradox, and from it he is still held back by his detachment, that self-protection which irony affords. The movement now required of him is a particularly spectacular one from his hesitant position, given an age as predominantly skeptical as the intellectual world of the 1920's. The slight movement which the poem makes is one of the reasons the poem proved so disturbing to the so-called Lost Generation. To make such a move was for Eliot to become vulnerable beyond Prufrock's anticipations of social vulnerability, for in that move intellect itself must accept its inadequacies and value reason more lightly. There is irony, then, in William Carlos Williams' accusation that Eliot's poem delivered poetry back to the academy; irony as well in the academic treatment of Eliot and imitation of him which have led reactionary critics like Karl Shapiro to charge that he is a bad influence upon criticism and poetry. For one could equally well make the charge, surely, that Eliot is anti-intellectual; Pound finds Eliot unreasonable in his growing inclination to the Church. But Eliot is neither anti-intellectual nor intellectual in the sense that those terms bear when used pejoratively. For how does one put intellect and reason in a proper relation to the self without denigrating them? It does not follow that they are rejected any more than it follows that the appropriation of the delicate, difficult, obscure (to the eyes of the modern world) thought of the past makes one "academic" in the pejorative sense. St. Augustine we remember writes his first signal work, after his escape of the desert, *Against the Academics.* (His explication of Genesis in *The City of God* and his long adumbration of the Word in Sermon 188 of *Sermons on the Liturgical Seasons* surely qualify him as a father of the New Criticism.)[1]

Eliot could never, not even in the beginning, give himself fully to irony. He could astound Bertrand Russell in that Harvard seminar with the remark that Heraclitus always reminded him of Villon. It is the sort of clever, shocking juxtaposition that uneasy brilliance hits upon, and it gave Russell pause to see Villon's restless passion beside Heraclitus' reflective statement of the permanence in change. (Russell returns to the event late in life but comments on it as if he at last suspects himself victim of a leg-pull. Earlier he "thought this remark so good that I always wished he would make another." But later when he asserts Eliot as possessing "an astonishing narrow-mindedness and intolerance," he remembers Eliot's statement as given in "a dreamy tone" and the only remark of the three-month course.) Wildean wit in a philosophy seminar at Harvard did not portend a Voltaire, for the role of Voltaire could not answer those discomforts of restless memory and desire in Eliot. He is too troubled by that matrix which awareness sustains and the questions attendant upon that state, questions which best reason does not solve but only thinks on occasion to have solved.

In that matrix, which Eliot was trying to order that he might extricate himself from it, there are immediate effects of ideas out of local history—typists and clerks, debris along the Thames. Ideas as immediate in *consequence* as one's physical response to the blare of taxis. The intricate motion and restlessness of industrial and social "progress," and the understanding of those causes through rational thought, trouble the heart of silence in the presence of whatever hyacinth girls. The contributions of Bacon, Hegel, Descartes—the spinning jenny or the throbbing engine of the body at tea or typewriter—are intricately present in the present moment of Eliot's awareness, whether or not he has sorted them out and rationalized them. To the extent one has not sorted them out, awareness and actions are on principles one is ignorant of. One's motions are but gestures, his journey a wandering to no end. We note at this juncture that Eliot's fastidiousness—his squeamishness about life in waterfront bars with sawdust and the litter of oyster shells, his fascination with the fisherman's world beyond that world's possibilities as simple metaphor—are not reactions simply out of a refined sensibility such as the young Aldous Huxley is surprised to find in Eliot (surprised, since Eliot is an American). The ambiguous address to the fisherman's world is very much out of a fear of being consumed by that life. There is a battle in Eliot in which his struggle for the unification of sensibility contends with the necessity of submerging the self in what Conrad calls the "destructive element" of the world if one is to accomplish the victory. The solution to the problem will prove destructive of one's intellectual pose, though not necessarily to the true intellect behind the *poseur intellectuel.* Eliot will be long in reconciling the lady of his "Portrait" or of "La Figlia che Piange" to that figure in the garden who goes in Mary's colors, as he will be long in coming to terms with the Sweeney in himself. That is, he will be long in coming to a proper love of existence, the multitudinous world, which must include himself. For there is in Eliot a very strong inclination to "neglect or belittle the desert." His awareness of this disparity, amusingly suspended in "Mr. Eliot's Sunday Morning Service" without a hint of solution to it, dictates the ironic mode and the necessity of a mask; there must be a "personality" or donnée provided to the poem to disguise the poet.

To come to a reconciliation with the desert is to have fully entered the country of paradox. There one is suspended by a dilemma requiring intellectual consent so that the statue of Priapus and the maiden and Mary come together in a still light on the threshold of yet another mystery, one larger than that of the individual awareness and including it. But before the climbing of the first stair of "Ash-Wednesday" there must be the unlocking of the door in *The Waste Land*.

Herbert Howarth, in his extremely helpful book, *Notes on Some Figures Behind T. S. Eliot* (1964), takes to task those who read the "light brown hair" lines of "Prufrock" as expressing disgust. But then he points to Eliot's use of Arnaut Daniel by allusion at the end of *The Waste Land* and suggests Daniel Eliot's pattern-figure. "Above all, [Arnaut] was the proper monitor for the anaphrodisiac poem because, the most illustrious love poet of his day, he leapt into the fire, *willingly*, to burn away his lusts." What Howarth doesn't emphasize is that Eliot's implied position is rather Dante's, dramatized through Arnaut. There is not disgust in the reaction to "light brown hair" in "Prufrock," but there is panic. And there is a deliberate attempt to regain composure by an intellectual distancing from those disturbing arms. When Howarth remarks that Eliot leaves America just before the Puritan strictures and suspicions of the physical gave way in the 1920's, the remark is important. But it is to over-read its importance to conclude that *The Waste Land* "does not make its effect by an *absence* of lubricity, but bids for a permanent abstention form lubricity, bids for the containment of our passions and dramatizes sexual experiences so that they seem painfully undesirable."

One must not finally conclude the poem an "anaphro-disiac" one. Howarth is surely correct that Eliot's use of Jessie Weston's *From Ritual to Romance* is "in definace of her argument," and it is true that the role of sex in the pub scene of the "Game of Chess" hardly makes it attractive. But in the poem's memory of the hyacinth girl at the beginning of the poem there is neither the panic of Prufrock nor disgust nor rejection. What one has is a sense of inadequacy, a sense of incompleteness in the relationship, with a lingering of desire. Human lovemaking isn't a sufficient cure of the soul's ills, as seems implied by Jessie Weston's reductions of ritual, any more than are Freud's solutions to the discomfort of anger, disillusion, and despair.

To refine Howarth's remarks so as to be closer to the mark, we may note that in *The Waste Land* we move from the condition of the late repentant in Dante's world upward to the top of Purgatory. We find that move in "What the Thunder Said." It is Eliot's double vision: Dante's mountain is placed in the present world, thus keeping it even closer to our literal world than does Dante, who found it necessary to place Purgatory a hemisphere away. Daniel's actions in Canto XXVI, his willingly burning away lust, does not imply the rejection of sex, but only a placing of it in its proper perspective. We should remember that lust is one aspect, not of love perverted (as is pride which is at the threshold of Dante's mountain) but of excessive love of the worldly. Eliot has moved beyond the puritanism of Origen—one of Augustine's principal adversaries—who in his single-minded concern for "Superfetation" of the One castrated himself as a protest against multiplicity. In "Mr. Eliot's Sunday Morning Service," Eliot has already seen that temptation, but sees as well its false direction. The irony of that early poem suspends action, but it cannot be suspended forever for Eliot. His desire is too strong.

It is the abiding spiritual dimension of the self which is crucial to Eliot at last and keeps desire burning in him. The spirit "feels" the necessity of a rescue out of the desert of history, though it comes to realize it cannot rescue itself by its own power. Since the time of Milton and Dryden, since the "dissociation of sensibilities," the laws of nature yield a power to the intellect such as reduces *person* to *individual;* that is the gnostic error of the modern world Voegelin adumbrates. But some higher law, Eliot came at last to believe after much agony, rescues the individual to his personhood again. The distinction here implied one may find argued at some length by Jacques Maritain in a little book first published at the time Eliot was issuing his essays *For Lancelot Andrews* and "Ash-Wednesday." In *3 Reformers,* after distinguishing the terms *person* and *individual,* with St. Thomas as authority, Maritain concludes: "as individuals, we are subject to the stars. As persons, we rule them." He goes on to ask and answer an overwhelming question: "What is modern individualism? A misunderstanding, a blunder; the exaltation of individuality camouflaged as personality, and the corresponding degradation of true personality." It leads to a "homicidal civilization." Thus Maritain in 1929, his attention focused on the spiritual dimension of our being, our particular person. Maritain's argument may be read as a complement to Eliot's early poetry, as a light upon that intellectual attempt to break out of the closed world of the self reflected in that poetry.

So we come in our own prelude to suggest once more that Eliot is of importance to us beyond the usual critical concern we encounter in the critical journals. Critical concern alas has been discovered to yield pragmatic return in the regions of secular power, in the world inhabited by the individual as opposed to the person. This is a realization upon which our own academy is now so largely built. The critical article, for instance, sustains the academic a moment longer as the academy itself collapses around us—because publication counts in a digital sense. In most universities, a man is his bibliography, and it is more important that words be printed than that the words signify. Little wonder that most academic noises appear, to the inquiring mind, as a strange whistling in the dark. What makes that whistling comically absurd, to the young in particular, is that it is a tuneless noise made for the most part by adolescent grey-beards. My playful trope here, you will remember, is a cliché that once applied to small boys who were forced to pass a graveyard if they were to get home. We seem to behold, more and more, old men uncomfortably confined in the graveyard of our civilization, having lost the journey itself—having (as Eliot says in a late poem) lost the voice of that Calling which alone may still the disquiet in us when we find ourselves in the graveyard of the self. Where our current ancients appear intellectually infantile and the young feel forced into the role of seer, it is difficult indeed to connect anything with anything. But Eliot, that young man trapped in a London bank, does not submit at last to despair when he recognizes the confusions we speak of. If on Margate sands nothing is to be connected with nothing, some new country still beckons. It is to that Calling as it appears in *The Waste Land* that we now turn.

"If Milton returned from the dead," says C. S. Lewis in his *Preface to Paradise Lost,* "and did a week's reading in the literature of our day, consider what a crop of questions he might bring you." Lewis is making a point we so easily forget when we are spectators of literature: that one must enter the particular world of the poem upon its own ground, including in part its historical ground, realizing that no work is so pure that it escapes the stains of its time and place or the personality of its creator.

Eliot, recognizing these threats to the poem he wished to write, attempts something very like Lewis' hypothetical resurrection of Milton. The attempt is made in part for dramatic purposes, but more importantly it springs from a deeply personal necessity, more crucial to Eliot than the rescue of his poem from the poet's personality or from his historical period. He conjured a mind remote from the modern world and forces its encounter with that social and spiritual chaos which Eliot himself is struggling to riddle. He imports to the center of his poem, not a blind poet, but a blind seer, and in that puzzled awareness whom he calls Tiresias, we find reflected the post-classical-Christian world in which Eliot has discovered himself such a restless alien. Not that Eliot's Tiresias asks a crop of questions directly; still, the questions are implicit in the disorder, in the fragmentation of a world suspended in a helpless, pagan consciousness. Those questions have to do with our reduction of life to a point that even the wisest of pagan seers is confounded by our progress in self destruction.

The cultural debris of the poem is that of both the Classical and the Christian worlds, the rubble of two decayed cultures from which there appears to be no exit for the trapped awareness. Eliot's note on his conjured ancient we know by heart: "Tiresias, although a mere spectator and not indeed a 'character', is yet the most important personage in the poem, uniting all the rest." The immediate advantage of such a strategy to the poem as poem is that it allowed the poet a control, a perspective upon that chaos of the modern world. Eliot had become so acutely concerned with the engulfing modern world that its impingement upon him caused what he referred to subsequently as a "nervous disorder." That circumstance notoriously accompanies his poem in our considerations of it. Indeed, that would seem to be the signal biographical point associated with our reading of it, second only perhaps to Pound's editorial contribution.

We might call the poem's point of view omnipotent, rather than omniscient. No walls arrest that floating presence Tiresias, who is not even a "character." Yet no pattern seems possible in London's drift for the baffled seer. We have a disembodied pagan awareness, let us say, drifting through our world as spectator, through whom (presumably) a reader is to be drawn into the poem's depths. It is, as technique, an adaptation of a fictional device descended to Eliot out of Henry James, which we also see refined and applied to the conscious and subconscious by Joyce. But there is in Eliot's poem this difference: the acute awareness drifting the poem, which we may not fully divorce from Eliot himself, has a new experience but seems at first to miss its meaning. The poem's Tiresias is in a country which is more radically different from its country of origin than James's Christopher Newman is from European cultural decline or Stephen Dedalus from Dublin's paralyzed waste land. Inevitably, Eliot's alien spectator is baffled by the experience. In the disparity between Tiresias' latent hunger for worldly order, to which Jesse Weston's study may serve in a limited explication, and the surrounding and engulfing disorder of this strange new world, lies the ground of the poem's ironies and the possibilities of inference from them. For by the disparity, the poem creates tensions such as are necessary, as Eric Voegelin says, to our sense of existence, lest we be forever caught in a dream world. Existence, to quote Voegelin,

> has the structure of the In-Between, of the Platonic *metaxy*, and if anything is constant in the history of mankind it is the language of tension between life and death, immortality and mortality, perfection and imperfection, time and timelessness, between order and disorder, truth and untruth, sense and senselessness of existence; between *amor Dei* and *amor sui*, *l'âme ouverte* and *l'âme close*; between the virtues of openness toward the ground of being such as faith, hope and love and the vices of infolding closure such as hybris and revolt; between the moods of joy and despair; and between alienation in its double meaning of alienation from the world and alienation from God.

Now if, as in "Gerontion," we do not reach conclusion about the disparity between Tiresias' old and new worlds, we advance at least so far as to rescue some fragments shorn in this collision of worlds. If the tensions are not resolved, they are at least certified, and one may turn from the pitiable struggle of memory and desire, turn almost to rejoice in despair itself. The voice in "Ash-Wednesday" argues that

> Because I cannot hope to turn again,
> Consequently I rejoice, having to construct something
> Upon which to rejoice.

What we are concerned with here is the strategy whereby Eliot moves beyond the tensional suspension marked by memory's relation to desire, to a tension rooted much deeper in the soul. This new drama lies in a struggle within those depths between hope and despair. And we discover in retrospect that Eliot makes his drama through a poetic strategy which becomes decisive in his own rescue as a person; it becomes more than literary strategy. We may recall that in his early criticism, he argues very strongly that the *personal* must be excluded from the poem if *feeling* is to be controlled in the poem. But we find him writing his friend Bonamy Dobre in 1929 that feelings out of the deeps of *person* are crucial: "I doubt myself whether good philosophy any more than good criticism or any more than good poetry can be written without strong feeling. . . I am sure that any prose I have written that is good prose, is good because I have strong feelings. . ." The strategy he attempts in *The Waste Land,* however is to control feeling by using myth. It is through myth that a modern world is to be made possible to poetry.

Eliot's use of his spectator Tiresias, released for the occasion from Dante's *Hell,* is in part to counter not only personal feeling but his own reflective bent, a bent which at some point threatens the content of thought or the form of art with the intrusion of the personal. There is a tension between nostalgic reflection, that element so prominent in those poems up to "Gerontion," and the prophetic hunger for a rescue out of time past and future. That tension allows the emphasis in the poem to rest upon a present tensional moment such as Voegelin describes. For Eliot is inclined at this early date to dwell heavily upon memory in his attempt to rescue a moment out of the past into the present. (That is, incidentally, a symptom of our modernity, upon which is built a variety of profitable industries trading in nostalgia.) But we recall also that St. Augustine dwells upon memory; in memory he finds a proof of the existence of the soul, and in the soul a memory of God as its origin. God "deigns to dwell in my memory," he says.[2]

Eliot's playing of his conjured awareness, Tiresias, upon a present chaos gives at least the illusion of a counter presence, a frictional movement of dramatic immediacy. That dramatic tension is explicitly emphasized as the struggle between memory and desire; the poem's opening lines underline the point. But in the last section of the poem the attempt to reconcile memory and desire in the poem's floating awareness occurs in a land which is neither the ancient mythical-historical world of Tiresias nor the external modern world of Eliot's London. A significant change has occurred, following those echoes of St. Augustine's journey to Carthage in "The Fire Sermon."

The battle in Eliot himself between memory and desire is so fundamental that we suspect his dilemma an Augustinian one —a spiritual one—and the poem not shocking to William Carlos Williams' sensibility simply because it betrays poetry to the academics. Nor is the difficulty simply a psychological one, which Eliot himself seems to have wished it to be at the time.[3] Nervous disorders were de rigueur in the 1920's. But spiritual crises, unless they could be elevated by intellectual abstraction from the deeply personal to the individual level—to the level of the social and political—were embarrassing to any citizen in that community of enlightened intellectuals Eliot found himself cast among. Even had he seen his problem as purely spiritual in 1922, as he was to see it in 1928, he would have appeared shockingly naughty to call it that. Had Eliot announced a desire to become Christian, Anglo-Catholic, at that early date, the inhabitants of Lady Ottoline Morrell's select salon would no doubt have deprecated his lack of taste. By the waters of Leamon he sat down to weep, for how should he sing the Lord's song in a foreign land.

NOTES

[1]But compare also Matthew Arnold's uncomfortable awareness in "Stanzas from the Grande Chartreuse" (1855), in which he compares the "death in life" of the cloistered monk to the new estate of the spirit in the modern world. Arnold declares himself "Wandering between two worlds, one dead,/The other powerless to be born,/With nowhere yet to rest his head." He is like "a Greek/In pity and mournful awe. . . Before a Runic stone—," a state one compares to Tiresias confronting London, 1922.

[2]Considerable light on Eliot's poetry may be borrowed from Hans Urs von Balthasar's *Theological Anthropology*, particularly from his section entitled "The Fragmentary Nature of Time," initiated by an exploration of St. Augustine's reflections on memory in relation to time.

[3]Conrad Aiken tells an anecdote about Eliot just before the writing of the poem. He could no longer write poetry, and Aiken passed on something of the problem as it appeared from his discussing it with Eliot to a friend, Dilston Radcliffe, who was seeing the American psychiatrist Homer Lane. Lane's message: "Tell your friend Aiken to *tell* his friend Eliot that all that's stopping him is his fear of putting anything down that is short of perfection. He thinks he's God." Aiken says, ". . .when I told Eliot of Lane's opinion, he was literally speechless with rage, both at Lane and myself. The *intrusion*, quite simply, was one that was intolerable. . . .But it broke the log-jam." "The Anatomy of Melancholy," *Sewanee Review,* Winter 1966, 189.

XVI

GENTILE OR JEW, REMEMBER

Who then devised the torment? Love.
Love is the unfamiliar Name
Behind the hands that wove
The intolerable shirt of flame
Which human power cannot remove.

Little Gidding

In retrospect, we see that Eliot was talking as much about his own recent poem as about Joyce's novel when he said in his review of *Ulysses:* "[Using myth] is simply a way of controlling, of giving shape and a significance to the immense panorama of futility and anarchy which is contemporary history. . . . Instead of the narrative method, we may now use the mythical method. It is, I seriously believe, a step toward making a modern world possible for art." It has been the apparent absence of a narrative method in the poem that has given us such difficulty in entering it. How does one move from Tiresias to St. Augustine and beyond, in the absence of a narrative line to follow? And so the suspicion lurks behind our attempts that the poem lacks unity, that it is at best five trays of bright shards, the remnants perhaps of a great mosaic largely lost to us, but one which the archaelogical critic might some day reconstruct through his science, should he ever have the good fortune to recover those discarded fragments of the original manuscript. Almost as soon as the poem appeared, Conrad Aiken tells us that it "must be taken. . .as a brilliant and kaleidoscopic confusion." He concludes his review in *The New Republic* by saying that "We reach. . .the conclusion that the poem succeeds. . .by virtue of its incoherence, not of its plan. . . . We 'accept' the poem as we would accept a powerful, melancholy tone-poem." Eliot's attempt to employ myth is, for Aiken, a failure because there appeared no grounds common in those myths the poem invokes upon which the poet may meet a modern reader. Eliot "gives us, superbly, *a* waste land—not *the* waste land."

What I have been arguing is that the poem Eliot gives us in 1922 has a unity independent of the private manuscript poem now recovered to us; yet it lacks a completeness which not even the published manuscript can be made to supply. It cannot have completeness because the poet himself is so tenuously upon the edge of vision that he cannot yet reconcile memory to his gnawing desire, though his memory is deeper than "personality" alone can supply, in the psychological sense in which Eliot and Aiken hold the term in 1920. A decade later, Jung will have

deepened that term by introducing us to the idea of the Collective Unconscious, but already Eliot is struggling to discover those
deep rivers of our common humanity that bind us as persons to
the past and to each other. *The Waste Land* is best read as part
of that complete poem by T. S. Eliot called the *Collected Poems:
1909-1962,* and of that larger poem it may be said that it has a
dramatic completeness, if not an aesthetic unity. I should like
to pursue the distinction by considering that floating awareness
named Tiresias. "What Tiresias *sees*," Eliot tells us, "is the substance of the poem." But it is the nature of Tiresias' vision that
is our concern.

If a central problem in Eliot's poetry, up to *The Waste
Land,* is the reconciliation of memory to desire, we might here
reiterate the movement beyond this point. In "Ash-Wednesday"
those tensional pulls give way to *hope* and *despair;* it is as if we
have moved from some hell to some purgatory. For in the later
poem, we find the speaking voice at a new level in its attempt to
reach an accommodation to "the immense panorama of futility
and anarchy which is contemporary history." There is also another change apparent on the surface of the later poetry. The
sensual level of man's existence is addressed in a new way. One
discovers that Eliot is increasingly more comfortable in the
presence of the created world. There is a growing affection for
the things of nature, more openly expressed,and from this point
his tone is less melancholy. There is less evidence of that Virgilean pathos, the inclination to the "tears of things" which one
finds in the early poems like a fog curling around and clinging to
images.[1] The bodily senses threaten consciousness less now than
seems true in the "Preludes." The "brown hair over the mouth
blown" is not so disturbing as those arms downed with light
brown hair are to Prufrock, who reacts in panic to any distrac-
tions from thought by the senses. And the senses are rejuven-
ated, as they cannot be for Gerontion. The "bent golden rod
and the lost sea smell/Quickens to recover/The cry of quail and
the whirling plover." The eye now blinded by vision recovers
"forms between the ivory gates," those gates no longer guarded
by Sweeney. And "smell renews the salt savour of the sandy
earth."

It is in this movement from one relation to the created
world to another—from the world as sensed through reconsidered
passion in a Gerontion, or a Sweeney sans memory, to the world

as sensed by the speaking voice in "Ash-Wednesday" and the
Four Quartets—that Tiresias may be spoken of as baptized. Not
only is he, but he must be if the journey is to be continued to the
completion of Eliot's own version of a divine comedy, his treatment of man's troubled existence in the created world. Otherwise, our poet must turn to a more desperate country of the
mind, within that entrapment by the mind in its own existence,
the dilemma which agitates Eliot's poetry up to, and almost
through, *The Waste Land*. Indeed, there is just such a journey
into a desperate country in a long fragment excised from the
fourth section of the poem, "Death by Water," the only section
of the 1922 poem, incidentally, to which Eliot supplies no aid
in what he later called "the remarkable exposition of bogus
scholarship," his notes to the poem. The excised fragment,
which appears in the transcript of the original drafts of the poem,
emphasizes this fourth section as a turning point in the complete
body of Eliot's poetry.

A sailor speaks the deleted lines. He recalls setting out from
his comfortable New England port, our New World Ithaca, past
the neighborly Dry Salvages, on a journey that takes him to the
edge of the world. It is a journey inward also, as we might expect, though the passage is heavy with imagery from the world
of the senses. The speaker's trials are at the level of man's natural life on the dramatic surface, that level which is the founda-
tion of the pagan world which Jessie Weston argues as under-
girding the medieval Christian world. (Eliot's tribute to Miss
Weston in his notes has tempted us to overlook the poem's
suggestion that her reading of ritual and romance is not adequate
to the deepest hunger of our desire.) Eliot's ship is driven past
"the farthest northern islands" in a fate-doomed course, reminiscent less of Ulysses' journey into the other hemisphere and toward another world as recorded by Dante than of that journey in
Edgar Allan Poe's *Narrative of A. Gordon Pym*. At the edge of a
new revelation, Eliot's sailor reports an encounter with a world
where

> A different darkness, flowed above the clouds,
> And dead ahead we saw, where sky and sea should meet,
> A line, a white line, a long white line,
> A wall, a barrier, toward which we drove.

It is the seam between two worlds, a barrier against which the driven ship may be destroyed. But we are suddenly returned to a present moment, out of that threatening encounter, by the narrator's flippant remark about "Home and mother." We suddenly find ourselves at a cocktail party, where Eliot's strange mariner has been telling his tale. He has stepped aside from a threatening engagement with what a Martin Heidegger might well explicate as an encounter with Nothingness. Poe, in concluding Pym's narrative, gives image to just such an encounter, made somewhat more explicit by that blank white figure of man which looms at the brink of the abyss. "March 22. The darkness had materially increased, relieved only by the glare of the water thrown back from the white curtain before us. . . . And now we rushed into the embrace of the cataract, where a chasm threw itself open to receive us. But there arose in our pathway a shrouded human figure, very far larger in its proportions than any dweller among men. And the hue of the skin of the figure was of the perfect whiteness of snow." Pym breaks off his narrative at this point also, and the experience of nothingness is without conclusion.

The dramatic move in *The Waste Land* goes, however, beyond an encounter with the abyss, in a gesture which costs "no less than everything," as Eliot will say long after. Those words from *Little Gidding* explore the mystery of the restoration of the self after a complete surrender of the self. The acknowledgment made in "What the Thunder Said" is of the awful daring of a moment's surrender which an age of prudence can never retract, and in these words we have an epitaph upon the old Tiresias. The words are spoken to the heart, to the blood of the inmost self, which is no longer the self it once was, since it can now say the words. It finds itself now in a country whose descriptive details are heavily reminiscent of Dante's country in Canto IV of the *Purgatorio,* where the late repentants are sunk down in the shade of a massive stone, out of the heat and the glare on the mountain, to rest unaccustomed eyes. Dante's souls are not yet released by their own daring of a moment's surrender, a point which may help explain our feeling that the awareness at the conclusion of *The Waste Land* does not seem released by its experience, nor its discomfort resolved. (Incidentally, repentance in retrospect must always appear late, and true contrition must qualify one's emotional response to new-found hope to a degree somewhat short of enthusiasm.)

In that long, discarded version of "Death by Water," the New England fisherman encounters his pagan dimension. The worldly dimensions of his being force him, through the agency of the sea storm, beyond the "illimitable scream" of the world's weathers. The conclusion of that long section, which is then followed by the ten lines that stand as the public version, at Pound's insistence, has the sailor asking to be remembered. He adds

> And if Another knows, I know I know not,
> Who only know that there is no more noise now.

The speaker is left puzzled, aware that more seems implicit in his adventure to the sea's end than has reached the heart of his understanding. This modern journeyman, encountering mystery, can only say that he is baffled by something beyond the powers of empirical account. For how may one explain that prelude he recalls to the encounter with a "different darkness" at the barrier line?

> One night
> On watch, I thought I saw in the fore-cross trees
> Three women leaning forward, with white hair
> streaming behind, who sang above the wind
> A song that charmed my senses, while I was
> frightened beyond fear, horrified past horror, calm.
> (Nothing was real) for, I thought, now, when
> I like, I can wake up and end the dream.

Is this the effect of bad food in a dozing watchman? Odysseus' sirens calling to destruction? Certainly he remembers an effect upon his senses radically different from that of the girls and the gin in "Marm Brown's joint." There is at least a hint of encounter with a new dimension of being in the experience.

The dramatic development of this discarded section leaves the mariner in a state of mind very like that which Eliot develops with detached deliberation in his "Journey of the Magi," whose speaker too is uncertain whether life and death have been changed in their meanings by his adventure. He knows only that he is "no longer at ease here, in the old dispensation,/With an alien people clutching their gods." The encounter with the Word within the word unable to speak a word has left the speaker uncomfortably disoriented, a stranger in his own country.

Still the New England sailor's encounter is of a different sort. It is an encounter with life as emptiness. "Nothing was real." It is an experience within a world where at best, after being a fortnight dead, one's bones are picked clean and the bones themselves claimed by coral. The self enters the whirlpool into nothingness. The message that comes back in the bottle of the body —the sailor at the cocktail party—seems to be that the body is empty.

Yet "Death by Water" does not end with the word *whirlpool*. There is a break in the lines, followed by a faint echo of a New Testament exhortation. And that echo signals a profound action in the poem's consciousness, an action between the lines, but one which cannot be articulated. In lines discarded from the public version of the last section, "What the Thunder Said," Eliot speaks of a name through which one may cross the threshold between the world of the infinite "illimitable scream" into a silent world deeply resonant of a presence, a presence such as Eliot will conjure in the rose garden of *Burnt Norton*. The speaker of *The Waste Land* fragment calls for

> The one essential word that frees
> The inspiration that delivers and expresses
> This wrinkled road which twists and winds and guesses:
> Oh, through the violet sky, through the evening air
> A chain of reasoning whereof the thread was gone
> Gathered strange images through which I walked alone.

The word is not spoken, and the last three lines here express a state of "nervous disorder" in which a memory of one's uncertain reason haunts the gathered but unpatterned images. The present reason is inadequate to see order in the fragmentation. The lines echo Dante's first night on Purgatory mountain in such a phrase as "violet sky." Vision must aid Dante's reason, even as it must Eliot's own pilgrim reason.

There lingers in these lines the suggestion that the lost word is in the power of the speaker—that he might speak it, appeal through it, if only it could be remembered. The first three lines, however, anticipate that essential word through which restoration is possible, though the appeal to and through the word is still delayed. Nevertheless, in the final section of the poem in its public version our journeyman sailor, whose name is rather certainly T. S. Eliot, has gone beyond a narrative thread of reasoning, a step by step logic. That thread of discursiveness has been dissolved by the mystery of an act. He leaves the world of nature as seen under the old dispensation, at Margate Sands, and strikes out into mountain deserts that no map of London or of England will discover, a land which no Tiresias may enter without changing his being more essentially than merely shifting sexes. It is a departure into a country opened to Eliot largely by St. Augustine and Dante.

Dante is seldom invoked in the footnotes to the early part of the poem, though his great poem is pervasively present. Eliot notes two instances for "the Burial of the Dead," but then the notes turn to Ovid, Virgil, and to Renaissance England in "The Game of Chess." In "The Fire Sermon" there is an echo of Pia, the late repentant from Canto V of the *Purgatorio*, after which the pagan Augustine is recalled, in words remembered to us by the Saint in his own lament for his late repentance, that ever "modern novel" we know as *The Confessions of Saint Augustine.* At the beginning of "What the Thunder Said" we have crossed a threshold, though words and the Word with which to name that crossing are still elusive, even in the notes. But here Dante at last comes into his own as a light upon the poem. There is a citation of the *Inferno* from Canto XXXIII, deep down in hell, in relation to the poem's lines "I have heard the key/Turn in the door once and turn once only." The words cited are from Count Ugalino's recollection of hearing himself and his sons shut away from the world, a terrible imaging of the effects upon the self wrought by its turning inward to maintain itself. In Ugalino's story, we see the horror of pride which leads to the Count's eating the flesh of his own children. Dante attempts, through the report of such spectacle, to show perverted love—the love of self which leads inevitably to spiritual self-consumption. We should notice, however, that Eliot's verb in the line he footnotes with Dante's passage is in the perfect tense: *have heard.* And we should note as well the second passage in the footnote, a farewell to the Bradleyan dilemma of the closed self, a world which has seemed impossible of opening.[2] We are past that key turned once, whose action is self-incarceration. There has been another key whose turning to open the prison of self is implicit in "Death by Water," a key not simply in the command of the self.

We might at this point name the key, but Eliot is not quite

ready to come openly to rest upon that word which is to be the subject of the lovely lyric of Section IV of *Little Gidding*. There, Love is declared "the unfamiliar Name/Behind the hands that wove/The intolerable shirt of flame/Which human power cannot remove." What we notice in the final section of *The Waste Land* is a new disorder, wilder than that experienced by our observer Tiresias in the first parts of the poem. Now distortion advances to hallucination. There is that figure of the woman who draws her hair out tight and fiddles a whisper music, turning the world upside down in a jumble such as Salvador Dali might render. Having reached, it seems, the threshold of Purgatory, the poem's awareness is forced back toward Hell again, as if we were already experiencing a dark version of Heraclitus' paradox of the way up and the way down. The suggestion is that one is perpetually caught in that double movement. One engages experience out of time, but from within each moment of time, since each moment of awareness is possibly the spot where two dreams cross. But from neither of these dreams may one fully wake himself, as the New England sailor has thought possible. And whether one's movement in the vertical plane—if one may so speak metaphor-ically of it—is up or down is always cause for confusion, out of which only the intrusion of grace upon the moment makes rescue possible. For it is grace which for Eliot dissolves the closed world of the self.

The movement in "What the Thunder Said" is now down-ward again after a vision of the heart, into the world of nature and history—community and individual. Into civilization, the continuing but decaying body of the social, and the world of the individual self and its body, that continuing medium of sensa-tion and thought in time. It is a descent into the world of a pagan death in life. We even have in one image a detail recalled from that final view Homer gives of Penelope's suitors, where they hang like bats crying in the darkness of Hades. But the turning back to time and place is most conspicuously a return to that world drifting in a pagan present, across London Bridge and along the banks of the Thames and in the typist's room of 1920. It is the world to which we must always return after vision, whether we know our place in time as 1920 or 1976. In other lines Eliot discarded from the final section of his poem, a separate floating awareness, through its "feverish impulses," encounters a changed Tiresias. This new awareness has become sufficiently separated from the dead world to allow it to rise toward putting its lands in order, after its vision in the depths; and it gives a final recollection, echoing once more Dante's lost souls in the figure of

> A man flat upon his back [who] cried
> "It seems that I have been a long time dead;
> "Do not report me to the established world."

This discarded fragment also ends with an account of a drowning, in which there is "neither up nor down," where the lamenting creature remembers only "about his hair the seaweed purple and brown." It is the drowned Phoenician-Tiresias awareness of the first three sections of the poem, as seen in the new light of a vision turned upon the contemporary world.

And so we look once more at the record of that drowning in the public version. We much emphasize the exhortation to "Gentile or Jew" out of St. Paul, that pre-Christian struck blind on the road to Damascus. What Paul requires of us is the death of the old man that the new may be put on. In "Death by Water" we have moved beyond the waters of the pagan world to the possibilities of the self-restoring fire and water, a rebirth in Christ. We should not suppose that from Eliot's personal position his uses of the pagan world are simply historical or literary. The pagan world, as he is to argue in *The Idea of a Christian Society,* is a limited version of the All to the half-blind; it is a partial world that exists at every moment of time in which faithless denial prevents our vision. If one gain this vision of the Pauline man, the pagan world can be remembered only as one distorted by false vision, the sort of distortion of creation that prompted Dante to prepare a special place deep in Hell for the pagan visionary, among whom we find that old baffled seer who once "sat by Thebes below the wall" but in Dante walks "among the lowest of the dead," his head reversed on his shoulders. It is as if in the earlier sections of Eliot's poem his spectator has been released from Dante's Hell, not from Homer's or Sophocles' worlds, and finds himself in a modern version of Hell in which landmarks and allusions give the time and place as London in the 1920's. Still, when that awareness is baptized, when there is the beginning at least of a putting off of the old man that the new may be put on, the old is a continuing part of the memory, a continuing and disturbing presence in self-knowledge, like Tiresias' remembrance of his double sexual state. Only at the top of

Mr. Purgatory, in the waters of Lethe, does one lose the memory of the old man in Dante's version of our pilgrimage.

We have in Eliot's Tiresias a state of consciousness approximating the poet's, though it is given a semblance of separation from the poet's personalty. It is changed anagogically in "Death by Water." And, as the appeal of that mystery inherent in the existing world becomes increasingly insistent to the poet, the old problem of point of view in the poetry diminishes. In the poems that follow *The Waste Land,* excepting "The Hollow Men" which is a special case, Eliot progressively surrenders his own voice and person to his poems. A more personal relation between the poet's and the poem's voices begins to surround and devour the earlier work. The *Four Quartets,* for instance, is a more explicit revisiting of the earlier poetry than generally granted. The personal enlarges and turns outward upon a world whose border upon the infinite is no longer a thin white line toward which one is hurled in a threat of annihilation. Where it had seemed once that "Nothing is real," in a country whose outer boundary was at best one's skull, now the Word is discovered intrinsic in the world, in the infinite desert, including a special presence in the Self.

The signal move in the body of Eliot's poetry, then, occurs interline—between the pathos of the first seven lines of "Death by Water" and the recovery promised in the three concluding lines that echo St. Paul. The move is out of the closed world Eliot was trapped in by his phenomenological speculations—a world he will call pagan in *The Idea of a Christian Society*—and into the world of St. John and St. Paul. But that first turning on the stair out of self-entombment, the act of self-surrender which prudence cannot retract, is so deeply personal as not to be found in one's obituary. Nor can it be reported effectively to the established world of the 1920's. To call *The Waste Land* a "personal grouse," as Eliot comes to speak of it, is understatement which should not hide from us how crucial the personal is to the poem's universality. It is not simply a piece of autobiography, obviously. Any rescue from peril, whether that of Odysseus in the chopped seas or of Dante from a dark wood, always becomes personal. When it is a self-inflicted peril to the soul, and in an age which largely denies the very existence of the soul, the attempt at sacrifice out of despair is likely to be taken as grousing against bad luck, against a pagan fate at best. One may be ill-advised to make a great show of it, as Gerontion realizes. That is why the phrase "personal grouse" has about it an aspect of understatement, like that of the pilgrim words in "The Journey of the Magi." That baffled voice, after its arduous journey, we remember, can only say to the established world, in words befitting flat: "it was (you may say) satisfactory."

NOTES

[1]The Virgilean pathos is in part an inheritance from Matthew Arnold, I suspect. One finds it an explicit concern in such poems as "Stanzas from the Grande Chartreuse." The "last of the people who believe," the monks, give "no ease" to the "Last of the race of them who grieve," Arnold's generation. What remains is a "melancholy" as our inheritance, with no adequate explanation or solution. Eliot, setting a distance between himself and that melancholy after "Ash-Wednesday," sets a distance from Arnold also, in his essay on "Arnold and Pater" in 1930.

[2]Again we recall this important note: "Also F. H. Bradley, *Appearance and Reality*, p. 346. 'My external sensations are no less private to myself than are my thoughts or my feelings. In either case my experience falls within my own circle, a circle closed on the outside; and, with all its elements alike, every sphere is opaque to the others which surround it. . . In brief, regarded as an existence which appears in a soul, the whole world for each is peculiar and private to that soul.' "

XVII

NOT TOO FAR FROM THE YEW TREE

This is the use of memory:
For liberation—not less of love but expanding
Of love beyond desire, and so liberation
From the future as well as the past.

Little Gidding

At this point we may consider the implications of Tiresias as "the most important personage of the poem, uniting all the rest." One does not suppose that Eliot chooses his principal "personage" out of Homer or Sophocles or Dante, but out of all three, and if he serves to unite the other personages of the poem, the sources from which Tiresias is drawn are united in him. "What Tiresias *sees*," says Eliot, "is the substance of the poem." He is a medium whose principle is seeing, and it is that principle which is decisive. This line of reflection leads us to recall that, in Dante's version of the blind seer, he is punished in Hell for his blind presumption in prying into the future, being one of those whose head is turned backward on his shoulders to signify the twisted nature of his prying into time. He has come into his own in Hell; for, since his vision cannot transcend time, he shares appropriately the condition of the souls condemned to Hell, the conditions of time unredeemed: he knows the twisted past and can see the shortening future as doomsday moves closer. He cannot know the present since to know the present is to make it already the past, to be removed from it by the act of reflection. In short, Tiresias is in that condition of tortured failure which Pascal describes as our most typical state in this world:

> Let each of us examine his thoughts; he will find them
> wholly concerned with the past or the future. . . . The
> present is never our end. The past and the present are our
> means, the future alone our end. Thus we never actually
> live, but hope to live. . . .

But even should Tiresias's physical sight be restored, he would still be half blind. He very accurately represents the limitations of the pagan world, the world of the unreal city. The saint, not the seer, knows existence in a perspective such as that suggested by the medieval tapestry Eliot sets up for us as a measure of Ariadne's world and Aspatia's in "Sweeney Erect." For the two-dimensional tapestry does not mean that its creator lacked space perception but that time and space are put in the context of the timeless and spaceless. Augustine represents that double vision also; through *The City of God,* the city of man is put in such a context that one can see it as an unreal city, insubstantial and hallucinatory when taken in its terms alone. To lack an eye for either world, for either city, is to be half-blind, to be grotesque like Tiresias or Polyphemus; or like Eliot's Origen or his sapient sutlers of the Lord or Sweeney; like the clever intellectual such as young Aldous Huxley or Bernard Shaw, or the primitive D. H. Lawrence or Bertrand Russell.

This, then, is the level of the personal in Eliot's poem, a level not advanced very far if we do not go beyond speculation as to whether it is elegy for Jean Verdenal, dead at Gallipoli seven years before its composition, or whether a reflection of an erotic problem with Vivien, sick in mind and body. If we must read it as an elegy, which is one of the ways it may be read, we are on much firmer ground to read it as elegy for the self, for the old man that must be put off on the authority of Paul. *The Waste Land* pinpoints the necessity of self-love corrected. The self, dramatized through its responses to a reflecting world, moves from seeing only its own likeness in that world. *Light* and *seeing* are key concepts, substantive threads in the poem, centering in Tiresias, in a mind troubled by the opaqueness of its own eyes and consequently of the world. This is the world of sunlight on broken columns, of withered stumps of time, in which persons are objects at best, passive or mock-active, as in the portrait of a Belinda at her toilet in "The Game of Chess" or the rendering of Fresca in Eliot's discarded imitation of Pope. It is a world in which no Beatrice has appeared, a point made rather directly by Eliot, though he does not cite the analogue in Dante in his notes.

> "Speak to me. Why do you never speak. Speak
> What are you thinking of? What thinking? What?
> I never know what you are thinking. Think."

When we cast those lines against the ones spoken by Beatrice on Mt. Purgatory, to Dante who cowers helpless before her scorching eyes, we see that the response in *The Waste Land* can only be

> I think we are in rats' alley
> Where the dead men lost their bones.

In Canto XXI Dante the Pilgrim, caught in the agony of his new humility, is rebuked by Beatrice with authority, dignity, righteousness from her flowery world beyond Lethe. Dante is presently to be drowned to the old man by Lethe and rise renewed through Eunoe's healing gift of good remembrance of himself. But not before he is reduced by Beatrice (lines 1-12, Canto XXXI):

> You, there, who stand upon the other side. . . Speak up!
> Speak up!. . . What are you thinking? Speak up, for the
> waters have yet to purge sin from your memory.

The discomfort in the presence of the female is not out of hatred or fear of sex in Eliot's poem so much as from a feeling of complicity in unfruitfulness, reflected in the drawing room as in the pub. The tone in the response to the lady's insistent question, a question out of her own vacuity which denies significant response, is sardonic, and so it marks a movement beyond the note of panic in Prufrock's response to a phsyical presence. It is also beyond the note of despair struck with the hyacinth girl in "The Burial of the Dead" when Tiresias-as-male responds

> I could not
> Speak, and my eyes failed, I was neither
> Living nor dead, and I knew nothing,
> Looking into the heart of light, the silence.

Both passages associate the drowned, opaque eyes with a remembered experience; the association is reflective, in a poem whose point of view is studiedly a shifting one. The separation of a present awareness from a past awareness, and the casting of that past awareness in the third person no more provides a literal male lover for Eliot than a separate person is implied by Wordsworth's account of stealing a boat in his youth when he remembers in the third person that "there was a boy."

The separation of the self, which Pound says Guinicelli introduces into Western poetry, has already been practiced rather obviously by Eliot in that self-love song of J. Alfred Prufrock. Those who, like G. Wilson Knight, would explain the implication of Eliot's use of "brother" in some of the discarded lines might well bear that point in mind and read Eliot's poem in the light of the Epistles of John, one of Eliot's sources, in which the word

brother is rather important, as is the concern with the eye's seeing a new light.   "He that loveth not his brother abideth in
death" (I John 3:14).   But it is "our heart [that] condemns
us" (3:20).   The heart of the male voice in "The Game of Chess"
is well along the way to conscious self-judgment, to self-condem-
nation, for the tone suggests a severe turning inward such as
Dante is forced to make before he can erase the memory of sin
with the waters of Lethe.   We look into the heart of darkness
which is the inclusive darkness the poem tries to dispel.   Pound's
objection to the use of a quotation from Conrad as epigraph to
the total poem, on the grounds that Conrad isn't "weighty
enough to stand the citation," misses this point, being concerned
it would seem with Conrad's reputation rather than with the
substance of the words Eliot chose.   Or if not that concern,
Pound may have glimpsed briefly the real point of divergence
with Eliot which will lead them increasingly down different
roads.   It is the substantive relevance that has led Eliot to the
Conrad passage:

> Did he live his life again in every detail of desire, tempta-
> tion, and surrender during the supreme moment of com-
> plete knowledge.   He cried in a whisper at some image,
> at some vision,—he cried out twice, a cry that was no
> more than a breath—
> > "The horror! The horror!"

Conrad's passage fits the poem's movement precisely, and
better than the substantive burden of the quotation from the
Satyricon which Eliot attaches as epigraph to the public version.
For it ties the modern world more closely to Dante's vision.
The Waste Land dramatizes the attempt to move off the point
of suspended spiritual death which Eliot saw as pervasive; it attempts to overcome that balance between memory and desire
that prevents movement and so requires of the awareness, like
Prufrock's or like Marlowe's speculative rendering of Kurtz,
that it live again every detail of desire, temptation and surrender
through the memory, as one is said to do when he drowns into
death.   That is a necessity which will be described in *Little
Gidding* as the last gift reserved to age, through which gift the
old man is put off that the new may be put on:

> the rending pain of re-enactment
> Of all that you have done and been; the shame

of motives late revealed, and the awareness
Of things ill done and done to other's harm
Which once you took for exercise of virtue.

Only then may memory be put in its rightful place, as Dante does at the top of Purgatory Mountain. It is an attempt to get beyond the illusion of movement which a literal geography and literary and social history provide a surface for in *The Waste Land.* And it does so, because for a moment it comes to see desire, temptation, and surrender in a light whose source is not itself.

It is here that we come once more to the center of the poem's personal dimension. The key lines are very near the end, where the voice of the poem pauses to speak from and to its heart of darkness, the "brother" and "friend" inside itself and deeper than either memory or desire. Once more it is a matter of self-address, but we notice that it is with a tone which is beyond the sardonic quality present in "The Game of Chess":

My friend, blood shaking my heart
The awful daring of a moment's surrender
Which an age of prudence can never retract
By this, and this only, we have existed
Which is not to be found in our obituaries.

What is acknowledged is an act which history cannot record, because it is not in time or place. We might recall that the lines are from that section of the poem which Eliot declares to Bertrand Russell shortly after publication "the only part that justifies the whole," a statement at variance with Pound's defense of the drowned Phoenician. The original version of these lines makes even more clear that we are engaged in a moment of self-knowledge such as Kurtz pursued in a more spectacular manner toward those headwaters on a dark continent. Kurtz brought back from his journey only the faint cry of Oedipus at the moment of complete knowledge. Eliot's lines originally are

My friend, my blood friend, beating in my heart,
The awful daring of a moment's surrender
Which an age of prudence cannot retract—

It is a moment of honesty in which the speaking voice meets the consequence of its failure openly, as Gerontion has insisted necessary. Eliot wanted to use "Gerontion" as a preface to *The Waste Land,* a proposal which Pound strenuously opposed. That Pound opposed such a juxtaposition of the two poems does not prevent its being a preface, and as such it stands as a summary of the burden of self-knowledge the journey of *The Waste Land* expands upon, just as "The Hollow Men" describes the empty spiritual country which is the point of departure for the other two poems.

In "What the Thunder Said," one has an articulation of an action which has actually preceded it. The words can be used to remember the awful daring of a moment's surrender, but only after that moment. If we are to locate the point in this shifting mind where the key is turned which releases the little world of the self from the Bardleyan dilemma, we will have to say it occurs in the closing lines of "Death by Water," lines which announce the gift of a key from a transcendent source. The moment of giving in which desire, temptation, surrender are made cannot be recorded in time's obituary. It is the moment of Pascal's great gamble, which throws one suddenly into an upside-down world such as he has not known before but which he finds less topsy-turvy as his eyes and sense of balance adjust to it. The sensation of the spirit is the reverse of that Dante suggests in the third section of his poem, where the soul ascending to the pure light rises but with no sense of movement such as the body invariably has. Eliot in contrast intensifies the burden of the senses. The eyes which have been turned inward in Eliot's poem are still turned downward, seeing towers upside down, hearing voices singing out of empty cisterns and exhausted wells. In a sequence which is chronological, but itself upside down to the new eyes as if it represents a regression, we tell over the fallen names Jerusalem, Athens, Alexandria, Vienna, London—all unreal.

The gamble cannot be said, it must be made. In a footnote to the final section of the poem, Valerie Eliot tells us that Eliot in a particular passage of his essay on Pascal's *Pensées* (1931) is remembering his own experience in composing the final section of *The Waste Land.* Eliot remarks in that passage of his essay that it is "a commonplace that some forms of illness are extremely favourable, not only to religious illumination, but to artistic and literary composition. A piece of writing meditated, apparently without progress for months or years, may suddenly take shape and word; and in this state long passages may be produced which require little or no retouch." Eliot is speaking with calm reflection on Pascal's conversion. From what we have said in these pages we may conclude that the conditions of his psycho-physiological troubles were extremely favorable to the writing of a poem which was both religious illumination and literary composition. We are not surprised that in his essay he does not draw the parallel between himself and Pascal. But one cannot read the essay carefully without seeing that it constituted one of those Plutarchian biography-autobiography pieces we have discussed. The parallels between Eliot's own spiritual history and that of his subject are everywhere implicit. The mathematician compared to the philosopher, in respect to the question of conversion; the imaginative journeyman of the incomplete *Pensées* as compared to the imaginative journeyman of the incomplete *Waste Land.* In his remarks on Pascal's middle-class, intellectual origins we see also reflections by Eliot upon his own background, some of which is recorded in those fragments of *The Waste Land* we have examined.

Nor could it be very far from his mind that the revitalizing experience of Pascal's life that leads him to the *Pensées* occurred at a point in time parallel to that in his own life when he wrote his most famous poem. Even on minor points there is a concern for parallels, as when he observes that Pascal composed "slowly and painfully, and revised often." And he may well have had in mind his own *Waste Land* when he calls our special attention to Sainte-Beuve's characterization of the *Pensées* as "a tower of which the stones have been laid on each other, but not cemented, and the structure unfinished," and apt analogy to *The Waste Land.* His own analogy of Jansenism as "morally a Puritan movement within the Church" with "its standards of conduct. . . at least as severe as those of any Puritanism in England or America" surely remind one of Eliot's own intellectual and moral origins and of a certain cast of mind that continued with him to the end.

Part V of his poem seems to have been composed spontaneously, and in speaking of Pascal he says, "he to whom this happens assuredly has the sensation of being a vehicle rather than a maker." That experience was rather certainly a high point in his career as a poet, surely one in which he escaped if but briefly the meticulousness of the mind composing. He did not enjoy the same degree of spontaneity before that point in the writing of his poems, nor afterward.   But his concern for form, which so troubles him with *The Waste Land*, from this point forward does not show the same degree of agitated experiment.   The fragments from *Murder in the Cathedral* issue naturally upon *Burnt Norton* as an enlargement.   The first of the *Quartets* does not require our seeing it in the sequence of a mind's movement toward the light in such a way that we must displace it from its historical publication, as we move the "Hollow Men" before *The Waste Land*.   Nor did it require the editorial help of a Pound to bring it to shape.   With the *Four Quartets*, Eliot moves beyond "poetry" as he had conceived it earlier, although he writes in verse.   For poetry was to him, in the struggle in which *The Waste Land* is so signal an event, an act which exhibits a sort of Heisenbergian "Principle of Uncertainty" in which there is a struggle with words as they slip, slide, dissolve under the very act of controlling and directing them.   The rebellion in favor of Chaos has its cause in an intellectual and spiritual inadequacy of the mind. It is as if when the poet ceases to be that "romantic" poet Eliot talks so often of, when he becomes comfortable in that double vision such as Augustine adumbrates in his explication of the word within the Word in his *Sermons on the Liturgical Seasons,* he is no longer the poet.   That struggle for freedom, which is the burden of the romantic's cry, is a struggle toward silence.   Parain, in commenting on that paradox of language, remarks that

> The ridiculous thing about life is that only death delivers
> us up to true solitude, and hence to true freedom. . . .
> Only and oddly, when we make silence in ourselves,
> what we almost immediately perceive is our dependence.

One adds that at that moment we fall victim to the excruciating desire to bear witness to that silence and are therefore reduced once more to words, as Augustine at Ostia found it necessary to turn "back again to the noise of our mouths." What a mind such as Eliot's might wish to add to Parain's concern with the poet's pursuit of that freedom which dooms his words (freedom, and the belief that such freedom lies only in death) is that Parain's is a conception of death at the pagan level. The one kind of death which answers the problem of freedom and sees it as a state other than oblivion is the one St. Paul describes as a putting off of the old man so that the new may be put on. St. Paul describes a condition of surrender, requiring continually no less than every-thing, as Eliot will assert as necessary at the end of his last signifi-cant poem, *Little Gidding*.

Long ago Eliot had spoken of surrender. In "Tradition and the Individual Talent," he was concerned with the poet's condi-tion in the act of composing. The process of creation requires of him "a continual surrender of himself as he is at the moment to something which is more valuable. The progress of an artist is a continual self-sacrifice, a continual extinction of personality." After *The Waste Land*, he sees those words as true but more largely true than he had imagined. Every moment is one re-quiring continual surrender to something more valuable even than the poem he may write in consequence of his gift. If *personality* is extinguished for the sake of poetry, it may be ex-tinguished for the sake of *person* as well, through a giving which involves a continual act of spiritual rescue by grace's descent into the opened, continually new person. At each point in that way one might find himself in a condition Eliot's Prayer Book describes. In "The Collect for Peace" one learns that to give, sympathize, and control is in the service of perfect freedom. The journey from Prufrock's tea party to *The Cocktail Party* is still not a narrative, still not a journey; it is the shadings of a mind continually turning to the light and so enlightened, and at every moment threatened by darkness. If *The Cocktail Party* is Eliot's compromise with silence and a memorial to the romantic poet he was, it is no mean service, even though not spectacular. Eliot's is finally a quiet voice, the voice of one who has realized, as he puts it in *Dry Salvages*, that most of us

> are only undefeated
Because we have gone on trying;
We, content at the last
If our temporal reversion nourish
(Not too far from the yew-tree [the living church])
The life of significant soil.

BIBLIOGRAPHY

Allen, Gay Wilson, and Clark, Harry Hayden, eds. *Literary Criticism: Pope to Croce.* Detroit: Wayne State University Press, 1962.

Antrim, Harry T. *T. S. Eliot's Concept of Language.* Gainesville: University of Florida Humanities Monograph Number 35, 1971.

Augustine. *The City of God.* Tr. by Walsh, Zema, Monahan, and Honan. Abridged by Vernon J. Bourke. New York: Doubleday and Company, Inc., 1958.

—. *The Confessions.* Tr. by John K. Ryan. New York: Doubleday and Company, Inc., 1960.

—. *The Essential Augustine.* Ed. by Vernon J. Bourke. New York: New American Library, 1964.

Barnett, Lincoln. *The Universe and Dr. Einstein.* New York: Bantam Books, 1968.

Bhagavad Gita. Tr. by Juan Mascaro. Baltimore: Penguin Books, 1962.

Bloom, Harold, ed. *Romanticism and Consciousness.* New York: W. W. Norton, Inc., 1970.

Dante. *The Divine Comedy.* Text with tr. by Geoffrey L. Bickersteth. Cambridge: Harvard University Press, 1965.

—. *The Divine Comedy.* Tr. by John Ciardi. New York: New American Library, 1954, 1961, 1970.

—. *The Divine Comedy.* Tr. by Dorothy L. Sayers. Baltimore: Penguin Books, 1949, 1955, 1962.

D'Arcy, Martin C. *Humanism and Christianity.* New York: World Publishing Company, 1969.

Day, Robert Adams. *Joyce's Waste Land and Eliot's Unknown God.* Pp. 137-210 of Literary Monographs, Vol. 4, ed. by Eric Rothstein. Madison: University of Wisconsin Press, 1971.

Drew, Elizabeth. *T. S. Eliot: The Design of His Poetry.* New York: Charles Scribner's Sons, 1949.

Einstein, Albert. *Relativity: The Special and General Theory.* Tr. by Robert W. Lawson. New York: Crown Publishers, Inc., 1961.

Eliot, T. S. *Collected Poems: 1909-1962.* New York: Harcourt, Brace & World, 1963.

—. *The Idea of a Christian Society.* New York: Harcourt, Brace and Company, 1940.

—. *Knowledge and Experience in the Philosophy of F. H. Bradley.* New York: Farrar, Straus & Company, 1964.

—. *On Poetry and Poets.* New York: Noonday Press, 1961.

—. *Notes towards the Definition of Culture.* New York: Harcourt, Brace and Company, 1949.

—. *Poems Written in Early Youth.* London: Faber & Faber, Limited, 1967.

—. *The Sacred Wood: Essays on Poetry & Criticism.* New York: Barnes & Noble, 1960.

—. *Selected Essays.* New York: Harcourt, Brace and World, 1960.

—. *To Criticize the Critic.* New York: Farrar, Straus and Giroux, 1965.

—. *The Use of Poetry and the Use of Criticism.* London: Faber & Faber, Limited, 1964.

—. *The Waste Land: A Facsimile and Transcript of the Original Drafts, Including the Annotations of Ezra Pound.* Edited by Valerie Eliot. New York: Harcourt Brace Jovanovich, Inc., 1971.

The Empiricists: Locke, Berkeley, Hume. New York: Doubleday and Company, Inc., n.d.

Feinberg, Barry, and Kasrila, Ronald, eds. *Dear Bertrand Russell. . .A Selection of His Correspondence with the General Public: 1950-1968.* Boston: Houghton Mifflin Company, 1969.

Firchow, Peter. *Aldous Huxley: Satirist and Novelist.* Minneapolis: University of Minnesota Press, 1972.

Gallup, Donald. *T. S. Eliot: A Bibliography.* London: Faber & Faber, Limited, 1969.

Gardner, Helen. *The Art of T. S. Eliot.* New York: E. P. Dutton & Company, Inc., 1959.

Gill, Eric. *Beauty Looks after Herself.* New York: Sheed and Ward, 1933.

Gross, Harvey. *Sound and Form in Modern Poetry.* Ann Arbor: University of Michigan Press, 1968.

Howarth, Herbert. *Notes on Some Figures behind T. S. Eliot.* Boston: Houghton Mifflin Company, 1964.

Huxley, Aldous. *Antic Hay.* New York: Random House, 1951.

—. *Crome Yellow.* New York: Bantam Books, 1959.

—. *Letters,* Edited by Groven Smith. New York: Harper & Row, Publishers, 1969.

Huxley, Julian, ed. *Aldous Huxley: A Memorial Volume.* London: Chatto & Windus, 1965.

James, Henry. *English Hours.* New York: Horizon Press, 1968.

Jung, Carl G. *The Portable Jung.* Tr. by R. F. C. Hull; ed. by Joseph Campbell. New York: The Viking Press, 1971.

Kenner, Hugh. *The Pound Era.* Berkeley and Los Angeles: University of California Press, 1972.

—. *T. S. Eliot: A Collection of Critical Essays.* Englewood Clifs, N. J.:

Prentice-Hall, 1962.

Kirk, Russell. *Eliot and His Age: T. S. Eliot's Moral Imagination in the Twentieth Century.* New York: Random House, 1972.

Kockelmans, Joseph J., ed. *Phenomenology: The Philosophy of Edmund Husserl and Its Interpretation.* New York: Doubleday and Company, Inc., 1967.

Levy, William Turner, and Scherle, Victor. *Affectionately T. S. Eliot: The Story of a Friendship: 1947-1965.*

Lewis, Wyndham. *Time and Western Man.* Boston: Beacon Press, 1957.

Maritain, Jacques. *Challenges & Renewals: Selected Readings.* Ed. by Joseph W. Evans and Leo R. Ward. Cleveland, Ohio: World Publishing Company, 1966.

Matthiessen, F. O. *The Achievement of T. S. Eliot.* Third Edition, with an additional chapter by C. L. Barber. New York: Oxford University Press, 1959.

Montgomery, Marion. *Ezra Pound: A Critical Essay.* Grand Rapids: William B. Eerdmans, 1970.

—. *The Reflective Quest for Order in Dante, Wordsworth, Keats, Eliot and Others.* Athens: University of Georgia Press, 1973.

—. *T. S. Eliot: An Essay on the American Magus.* Athens: University of Georgia Press, 1970.

Newman, James R., ed. *What Is Science?* New York: Washington Square Press, Inc., 1955.

Niemeyer, Gerhart. *Between Nothingness and Paradise.* Baton Rouge: Louisiana State University Press, 1971.

Parain, Brice. *A Metaphysics of Language.* New York: Doubleday and Company, Inc., 1969.

Pascal. *Pensées.* Tr. by A. J. Krailsheimer. Baltimore: Penguin Books, 1966.

Pound, Ezra. *The Cantos.* New York: New Directions, 1970.

—. *Letters.* Ed. by D. D. Paige. New York: Harcourt, Brace & World, 1950.

—. *Personae.* New York: New Directions, n.d.

—. *The Spirit of Romance.* New York: New Directions, n.d.

Russell, Bertrand. *The A B C of Relativity.* Third Revised Edition, ed. by Felix Pirani. New York: New American Library, 1958.

—. *The Autobiography: 1914-1944.* Boston: Atlantic Monthly Press, 1967.

—. *The Autobiography: 1944-1969.* New York: Simon and Schuster, 1969.

Reid, B. L. *The Man from New York: John Quinn and His Friends.* New York: Oxford University Press, 1968.

Robinson, Forrest G. *The Shape of Things Known: Sidney's Apology in Its Philosophical Tradition.* Cambridge: Harvard University Press, 1972.

Science News. Washington, D. C.: Science Service, Inc.

Sencourt, Robert. *T. S. Eliot: A Memoir.* Ed. by Donald Adamson. New York: Dodd, Mead, 1971.

Smith, Grover. *T. S. Eliot's Poetry & Plays: a Study in Sources and Meaning.* Chicago: University of Chicago Press, 1960.

Tate, Allen, ed. "T. S. Eliot (1888-1965): A Special Issue," *The Sewanee Review,* Vol. 74, No. 1, January-March, 1966.

Vivas, Eliseo. *Creation & Discovery.* Chicago: Henry Regnery Company, 1955.

Voegelin, Eric. *From Enlightenment to Revolution.* Ed. by John H. Hallowell. Durham: Duke University Press, 1975.

—. *Israel and Revelation.* Vol. I of *Order and History.* Baton Rouge: Louisiana University Press, 1957.

Weston, Jessie L. *From Ritual to Romance.* New York: Doubleday and Company, Inc., 1957.

Whitehead, Alfred North. *Modes of Thought.* New York: G. P. Putnam's Sons, 1958.

—. *Process and Reality.* New York: The Macmillan Company, 1929.

—. *Science and the Modern World.* New York: The Macmillan Company, 1925.

—. *Symbolism: Its Meaning and Effect.* New York: G. P. Putnam's Sons, 1959.

Eliot's Reflective Journey to the Garden

Composed in IBM Selectric Composer *Journal Roman* and printed offset, sewn and bound by Cushing-Malloy, Incorporated, Ann Arbor, Michigan. The paper on which the book is printed is The Northwest Paper Company's *Caslon*.

Eliot's Reflective Journey to the Garden is a Trenowyth book, the scholarly publishing division of The Whitston Publishing Company.

This edition consists in 500 casebound copies.